The Story Behind

"In Broad Daylight"

By

HARRY N. MACLEAN

BOOKS BY HARRY N. MACLEAN

The Joy of Killing
A Novel

The Past Is Never Dead
*The Trial of James Ford Seale and
Mississippi's Struggle for Redemption*

Once Upon A Time
A True Story of Memory, Murder and the Law

In Broad Daylight
A Murder In Skidmore, Missouri

INTRODUCTION

On July 10, 1981, Ken Rex McElroy was shot to death as he sat in his Silverado pickup on the main street of Skidmore, Missouri. At least forty-five people witnessed the shooting. McElroy's wife, Trena, who was sitting next to him, identified the primary shooter. In spite of three grand jury investigations, no indictments were issued.

McElroy, who had visited a reign of terror on Nodaway and surrounding counties for more than twenty years with near impunity, had been convicted in 1980 of assault for the shooting of an elderly grocer in the neck. That July morning he was scheduled to appear at a bond revocation hearing because of an incident a few weeks earlier in which he had carried a rifle into the D & G Tavern. Anticipating trouble, roughly sixty-five men had gathered in town the morning of July 10 to form a parade of pickups to escort the four men who were going to testify against him safely to the courthouse in Bethany, a small town about seventy miles east of Skidmore, where he had been tried and convicted of the assault.

What most of the men gathered didn't know was that the hearing had been postponed. The afternoon before the hearing, McElroy's lawyer filed a motion to delay it to a later date, which was granted by the judge. When news of the continuance reached the men in town, they congregated in the Legion Hall to talk and figure out their next move. News of the meeting reached McElroy. He drove into town with his wife, parked in front of the D & G Tavern, and went inside. Word that McElroy was in town spread quickly, and before long the men in the Legion Hall poured out of the building and down the hill to confront him. Fifteen or twenty men went in the tavern. The others gathered in the street. A short time later, McElroy and his wife left the tavern and got in their truck. Shots rang out from across the street, and McElroy's head fell forward onto his chest, his skull shattered. There he lay for well over an hour, until his brother Tim called his Kansas City attorney, who finally called the county sheriff.

The national press ran with the story as an Old West "vigilante killing of a town bully." The weekly news magazines carried pictures of McElroy holding a small girl and staring malevolently into the camera. I—along with millions of others—was fascinated by the story. How could McElroy have gotten away with his string of crimes for as long as he did? How did the shooting come about that morning? And finally, how could the forty-five witnesses have maintained their silence for so long?

At the time of McElroy's murder, I was arbitrating labor disputes in Denver, Colorado. Although I had long wanted to be a writer, I had never written anything other than legal briefs and opinions and an occasional newspaper column. I knew that many writers would be descending on the town for the "real story." I also knew that the town would be locked down tight and that outsiders would be less than welcome. Nonetheless, the story proved irresistible. A year after the shooting, I finally loaded up my car and headed east across the plains to Skidmore,

Missouri.

Six years later, "In Broad Daylight" was published. The reality far exceeded the dream. The book was a New York Times bestseller, won an Edgar Award, and was made into a movie. As I traveled and talked about the book, I realized that there was almost as much interest in how I got the story as in the story itself. How did I get people to talk? Was I ever scared? How long was I there? Did I know who killed Ken McElroy? What was the town like now?

When the thirtieth anniversary of the killing approached, I decided there should be an informal commemoration of the event. On July 10, 2011, I met on Skidmore's main street with Jeffrey Dalsing, one of McElroy's lost children, and several others in town who had helped with the book or been part of the story. I also decided it was time to tell the story behind the book. The following is that story, told in the framework of the gathering on the town's main street on the thirtieth anniversary of the killing.

Author and Brian Denehey as Ken McElroy on the set of the movie "In Broad Daylight." Denehey captured McElroy so well he made people on the set nervous.

CHAPTER 1

July 10, 2011. Five or six of us stood in front of the Skidmore Café on the main street of town. It was thirty years ago to the day after Ken Rex McElroy was shot to death as he sat here in his truck. I had called a few people and posted a note on Facebook inviting others to join us at the café for coffee at 9 A.M., a little more than an hour before the shooting had taken place. I wondered if any friends of Del Clement—one of the alleged shooters—would show up. Several of them had been unhappy that both in my book, "In Broad Daylight," and in a blog I had written a year ago, I had described Del as a short, hot-tempered drunk. My guess was that they wouldn't make it.

Glancing about the street, I pictured what it had been like that morning thirty years earlier. For a few moments, guns were blazing. First, a .30-30 high-powered rifle, then a .22, and perhaps a shotgun. When the high-powered weapon opened, its shots shattered the air: Boom! Boom! The .22 would have snapped, like the crack of a whip. Some heard the explosion of a shotgun; others didn't. It was a hot day under the Missouri sun.

We were standing only a few feet from where the shooters stood. From here you could have seen the rifles come out of the window racks in the trucks and rise to the shoulders of the shooters. I wondered what the witnesses' first thoughts were as the glass shattered and the dark head slammed forward.

It was Sunday morning and the street was empty, except for our small group and a few men sitting at a table, drinking coffee, outside what used to be Sumy's gas station on top of the hill. The café used to be the post office, and the Quonset hut across the street, shuttered and for sale, used to be the Skidmore Café. In July 1981 it was the D & G Tavern for owners Del and Greg Clement. In all my years in this town, the only name I ever heard for the man on the .30-30 was Del Clement. McElroy's wife, Trena, seated beside him in the truck, told me in person and swore under oath more than once that she saw Del take the high-powered rifle from a red vehicle, aim it at her husband, and squeeze the trigger.

It wasn't hot yet, but you could feel the heat rising in the damp air. At this precise moment, the men would have been gathered in the Legion Hall a few yards up the hill, calculating what they could do about McElroy, who, having been turned loose on bond after being convicted of shooting the grocer in the neck with a shotgun, was now as dangerous as a wounded water buffalo. As the men poured out of the building and down the street to the tavern, they would have glanced at the two-tone brown Silverado and spotted the empty gun rack in the rear window. If they had had any idea what was about to happen, they would surely have climbed into their pickups and gotten the hell out of there.

I figured that someday, what happened here that morning would become a part of history, like the gunfight at the O.K. Corral or the murder of Jesse James. One day the great-grandchildren of the men on the street would stage a festival around a reenactment of the killing. Ken Rex McElroy Days. You could buy T-shirts with a shotgun on the front and his terrifying visage on the back. That is, if the town was still here; it had been in serious decline for years. Grocery store, gas station, tavern, bank: all closed.

The owner of the café had decided not to open on the morning of the anniversary. Not enough business, he said, and maybe he was right. No one wanted another incident. Locals hoped that the town's bad days were behind it, although Providence never seemed to give the place a break. A few years ago the national media had once again descended on the town as it mourned the death of Bobbie Jo Stinnet, a young pregnant woman who had been cut open and had her baby stolen from her womb by a deranged Kansas woman.

A successful true crime author who wrote a book on the Stinnet murder commented to me how surprised she was that she couldn't get anyone in town to talk about Bobbi Jo or anything else. You should have seen it twenty-five years ago, I wanted to say. Now the residents politely declined; then some had slammed doors in my face, or worse. The town had wanted badly to believe that if it just ignored the killing of Ken Rex McElroy, the whole thing would go away. Their resolute silence only made the story more compelling.

I left our small gathering and walked up to what used to be Sumy's station at the top of the hill for a cup of coffee. A reporter from the Maryville paper had shown up. The station owner, not an original local, asked me if I had a book for sale (which I didn't). I took a picture of those seated at the table, and walked a few feet in front of the station to the intersection, looking down the hill. Seven or eight of the men coming out of the Legion Hall that morning had swerved off and stood at this spot. From here, they would have had a perfect view of the entire episode: of the men walking down the hill and going into the tavern, of McElroy and Trena coming out and getting into the Silverado, of 20 or 30 men following them out and standing around the truck and up the hill, of two men walking to their trucks and reaching inside for their rifles.

Of someone shouting, "Shoot the sonofabitch!" Of the rifles blazing, of glass shattering, and a head exploding. Of a bloody, screaming woman being pulled from the truck and run up the sidewalk to the bank.

The men here would have seen it all without turning their heads. One of them, Frankie Aldredge, had told the law what he had seen. But after he received a visit from Del Clement's lawyer, his story changed. When I talked to Frankie in the eighties, he claimed not to have seen a thing; however, his original, signed statement to the police unequivocally identified Del Clement as the shooter.

Over the years, as the witnesses passed away, I had expected that one of them would confess on their deathbed to what they had seen. I figured good Christians wouldn't want to take that secret to the grave with them. So far, I was wrong.

Missouri, I had learned during my time here, was a strange place. Although next to Kansas and Illinois, it was neither the Great Plains nor the Midwest. Directly above Arkansas, it more resembled the South—it had been one of four slaveholding states that didn't join the Confederacy —yet you didn't see Baptist churches on every other corner like you did in some small southern towns. The Christian Church on the edge of Skidmore was fundamentalist, with a full-immersion baptizing tank on the altar, but its influence wasn't widely felt. There had been a beautiful redbrick Methodist church with stunning stained glass windows on the road into town. When the repairs became too costly, the congregation tore it down and replaced it with a dull one-story building. Now there was nothing pretty in Skidmore.

I couldn't see a small town in the Midwest letting its streets and buildings fall apart as Skidmore had. It was the same sort of attitude, I would sometimes think, that provided fertile ground for the likes of Ken Rex McElroy to rise from. Everybody takes care of his or her own business.

I looked at my watch: 9:50. Right about now, I figured, 30 years ago, the scene in the tavern was heating up. McElroy and Trena were sitting at the bar, not far from the door. The men stood around, drinking, talking, glancing at McElroy through the smoky air. A few played pool. Del and Greg Clement served beer from behind the counter. McElroy ordered a six-pack and a pack of cigarettes. Nobody knew what the next move was, but there had to have been a growing feeling of impending violence.

McElroy must have been enraged when he heard the town was having a meeting about what to do with him. "He never knelt down to nobody!" Trena said defiantly to the media in the days after McElroy's death, and, in fact, you could say that up until that day the town had more likely knelt down to

Maryville Daily Forum photo by Don Shrubshell.
The Silverado shortly after the shooting. You can tell the angle of fire from the shattered rear and side windows.

McElroy. So he drove into town, without his guns, his pretty young blonde wife at his side, to answer the affront. Trena said he never spoke a word on the drive in, but I suspect by the time he parked in front of the tavern and flung open the driver's door he was pleased that it was all finally coming to a head. He had sworn he would never go to prison. And he told others he didn't expect to live a whole lot longer.

CHAPTER 2

On the morning of the anniversary, David Dunbar was leaning up against the rail in front of the café, talking to Kermit Goslee, the second son of the Goslee family, with whom I stayed during my time in Skidmore. Dunbar had been elected town marshal a few months before McElroy was killed. He took his duties seriously, but not too seriously. Many evenings he sat on a stool in the D & G with his badge on his jean jacket, and drank with the locals. He kept his pistol in the glove box of his car.

Dunbar came from an Iowa town near the Missouri border, and had moved to Skidmore to work on the pipeline. He lived with his wife and two kids in a small house near the edge of town. He was handsome with an engaging smile, and women loved him. He had been a football player and a wrestler in high school, and he had maintained thick shoulders and arms. The Clements and their crowd didn't intimidate him.

Dunbar and I had eventually become friends. Along with Kermit Goslee, we caroused in clubs and bars in northwest Missouri and southern Iowa. One night in the Elks Club in Maryville, the Nodaway County seat, Dunbar and Del Clement had gotten into an argument over his association with me and gone outside to have it out. Clement backed down. In the early days of my presence in Skidmore, there had been a price to pay for being my friend.

Once Dunbar put the badge on, as a lark or not, whatever comity existed between him and McElroy evaporated. In the tavern, McElroy gave him that penetrating, baleful stare that kept people on edge or drove them from his presence. The day that McElroy pulled a shotgun on Bo Bowenkamp on the loading dock behind the grocery and blew half his neck away, Dunbar had been at a friend's house drinking beer. When he heard the commotion, he pulled himself together and investigated.

Dunbar would be called upon to testify at McElroy's upcoming trial for assault on the grocer, and McElroy was not pleased about it. McElroy had a way of getting witnesses to disappear or forget what they thought they saw—Trena's parents could swear to that. Although Dunbar hadn't seen the shooting, or even McElroy at the scene, he was part of the lineup of witnesses. McElroy understood fear: Scare one witness, one juror, one DA, or one judge, and the others got the message.

In the year or so before the shooting, McElroy had gotten worse, and most people stayed out of his way. It was just simpler not to have an encounter with him than to try to straighten it out later. Kids learned to get off the street when he came to town. He would stop in the tavern and drop a sack full of twenties and hundreds on the bar top and invite anyone there to help themselves. He might even insist on it. You could be in serious trouble either way. If you didn't grab some money, it might be because you thought you were too good for McElroy, that you were from one of the wealthy farm families who looked down on the McElroy family as a bunch of ragtag pig farmers.

The year after he shot Bo, the town was a like a powder keg waiting for the spark. Nobody wanted to be around when it happened. When McElroy's Silverado reached the edge of town in those days, the phone lines began buzzing, and by the time he parked in front of the tavern the whole town knew where he was. It was ruining business at the D & G.

For all intents and purposes, there was no law in Skidmore in 1981. The town was isolated; lawmen, with a few exceptions, weren't anxious to run into McElroy; and McElroy, who never made it beyond sixth grade, who didn't have a social security number and had never filed a tax return, knew the rules as well as they did. Lois Bowenkamp, Bo's wife, had been calling and writing the governor and the attorney general asking for help, but all she received were polite letters telling her it was a local problem. The other thing was, people in Skidmore weren't anxious to draw McElroy's attention to themselves by helping her. The local minister had stopped by the house to counsel Bo after his release from the hospital, and that very night he and his family received unwanted visitors. The minister began packing, and kept packing until the day McElroy was shot.

Standing in front of the café, 30 years after the shooting, I wondered if McElroy enjoyed this power over people, over the town, if he derived a perverse sort of pleasure from it, the cowering, or if he was simply caught up in the bloody dynamics of the drama. I asked Trena during our interview, and she couldn't say. I wasn't sure she really understood the question. Toward the end, she had become a fearsome character in her own right; tilting a shotgun out the passenger's side window, blonde hair blowing in the wind, as the Silverado led a line of McElroy pickups by the Bowenkamp or Dunbar house.

Dunbar had encountered Trena. The Punkin' Show in those days was the town's annual rite of community. For three days there were dances, tractor pulls, rodeos, bake-offs, frog jumping contests, beauty contests, barbecue competitions, parades, and lots of partying, in the tavern and on the streets. Skidmore, I always said, was not on the road to anywhere; you ended up there only if you wanted to go there. A lot of people came to town for the Punkin' Show. In the evening, a steady, slow stream of pickups rolled down the main street.

On the Friday night of the Punkin' Show in 1980, only a few months after McElroy had shot Bo and while he was awaiting trial, Dunbar sat at the bar in the D & G, with his badge on, drinking beer. As he was leaving the tavern, he heard a voice: "Hey, Dave, come over here a moment. I want to talk to you."

Dunbar knew McElroy's voice. "Fuck," he thought. "Here we go." McElroy was standing by his truck, in the gravel drive between the tavern and the back of the bank and the grocery store. The spot was in the shadows, a little out of the glare. Dunbar walked over. McElroy stared with glassy eyes at the badge on Dunbar's jacket.

"Are you going to testify against me?" McElroy demanded. "I have to," Dunbar responded. "It's my job."

"I'll kill anybody who'll put me in jail for the rest of my life," McElroy said. He reached in the bed of the pickup and swung a shotgun up and out into Dunbar's face. Dunbar grabbed the barrel and held it away from him. McElroy flicked his own right ear, and in his peripheral vision Dunbar saw a form begin to move behind him. Suddenly, he felt cold steel bite into the back of his neck. Trena was holding a shotgun to the base of his skull. Another flick of McElroy's finger and he was gone.

Dunbar eventually talked his way out of it. He reported the incident to the sheriff's office in Maryville, and was told there was nothing that could be done. Just keep an eye on him. The guy was pulling shotguns on the law in the middle of a festival and the sheriff's response was to say, "Keep an eye on him"? The next morning Dunbar walked to the gas station that had been converted to city hall and laid his badge on the table. Two hundred and forty dollars a month wasn't close to what it would take to go up against McElroy.

Now, on the morning of the 30th anniversary of the shooting, Dunbar recounted the story of his encounter with Trena and McElroy to the reporter and the small crowd that had gathered in front of the café. He added that by the time he got home that night he was really pissed, and he grabbed a rifle and got in his car and went looking for McElroy, but he couldn't find him.

A faded mid-90s gray car slowed as it passed in front of us. Twenty yards down the hill, it stopped, then swung around into a parking spot.

"Watch out," Dunbar said, "it could be an ambush."

He chuckled as he said it, but he kept his eye on the car, as did I, as did the others. McElroy still had a lot of family in the area—I had been in contact with some of his kids over the years—and more than a few fans and followers, some of whom considered him a sort of a Robin Hood because he stole from rich farmers and shared his ill-gotten booty with them.

Northwest Missouri was a more civilized area now than it was in 1981, when McElroy met his infamous end, but there was still an outlaw element here, and there were still a lot of bad feelings about what had gone on that summer, and how it had come to an end on the morning of July 10. The black car sat there, in the growing heat, its occupants invisible in the harsh light. Close to a minute passed, and Dunbar repeated his comment, without a chuckle this time. I kept my eyes on the driver's door, thinking it couldn't be good, someone sitting in the heat that long. Finally the door swung open.

CHAPTER 3

McElroy left many children, and some of them were unhappy with the way their father was killed and the way he was portrayed in the book "In Broad Daylight." Although, to be fair, I had not heard a hostile word from any of them. McElroy's many friends have also largely kept silent over the years. The friends of Del Clement, the man who by all accounts had opened up on McElroy with a . 30-30 a few feet from where we were standing, were another matter. They were none too happy that I had raised the possibility that Del might be a coward for shooting McElroy in the back. I had received a couple of semi-threatening e-mails.

I had several encounters with Del during my days in Skidmore. The first was at the large Clement ranch a few miles outside of town. The Clements and their friends were cowboys; they wore cowboy hats, rode horses, and carried rifles in racks in the rear windows of their pickups. They also rodeoed. The Clements had constructed a rodeo ring on their ranch, with chutes for calves, steers, and horses to sprint out of when the rope dropped.

In the summer of my second year in Skidmore, the Clements held a rodeo on their ranch. Word of the event went out all over northwest Missouri. Cowboys and cowgirls from as far away as Kansas City came with their ropes and horses to compete for modest prizes.

A few days earlier, I had spotted a flyer for the event in

the Skidmore grocery store, still doggedly run by Lois Bowenkamp. I thought long and hard about going. I had no reason to think Del or his brother, Greg—sometimes mentioned as the man on the .22—would talk to me. In fact, I had reason to think that Del, at least, would be overtly hostile. But you can't write a book about a killing and not at least try to interview the man widely believed to be the killer. If I called, he would certainly hang up on me. On the other hand, I didn't relish showing up at his ranch alone and uninvited. I had been to enough ranches and farmhouses in the area to know that the inhabitants generally spotted you long before you got to the door. The Clements had to know who I was and what I was doing. Maybe it was best to approach Del in a familiar setting with lots of people around.

When I showed up at the ranch on the day of the rodeo, pickups and horse trailers already packed the grounds outside the house. The rodeo was in full flourish: calves ran out of the chute, and cowboys on horses galloped after them, ropes spinning overhead. I leaned up against the fence with other spectators and watched. Del rode out in a fury and spun his rope out over the calf's head, but it slipped off and dropped to the ground. He sat on his horse, and swore as he twirled up his rope. I watched him leave the ring, dismount his horse, and tie him to a rail. I had practiced my approach: I was going to introduce myself and say I was doing some research on the killing that occurred here a few years earlier. I wouldn't mention McElroy's name. Not that it would fool him.

I took a step in his direction, and then a cowboy appeared at his side, and then another, and they appeared to be reliving his failed attempt to lasso the calf. He shook his head, tipped his white cowboy hat back, and wiped his forehead. (The hat, I noticed, gave him at least three inches. You never saw him without it on.) I didn't want to approach him in a group. I waited.

Finally, Del separated himself from the others and walked in the direction of a small barn about thirty yards away. I watched as he disappeared through the door. I walked toward the building, reciting my opening line. I entered the door. Hay bales were stacked in one corner. Bridles and leather straps hung from a wall. Del was kneeling down, fooling with something on the floor. I said his name. He stood and turned. He was a good-looking man, with a steady, direct gaze. I introduced myself, and said I was a writer from Denver, Colorado, doing research into the killing in Skidmore.

"You need to get off the ranch," he said, eyes hardening.

"I'm not really trying to solve the killing or figure out who the killer was. I'm trying to tell the story from the town's perspective. I . . ."

"Maybe you didn't hear me," he interrupted. "If I was you, I'd get off the ranch, right now."

I thought of trying another line, but his eyes and the tightness of his face persuaded me otherwise. It was a mistake, I saw, to come on his ranch. It was an invasion of his privacy. Things could go bad real quick.

"OK," I said. "I'm leaving." I backed up the few steps to the door, turned, and began walking across the property to where my car was parked. It seemed a damn long walk. I hadn't seen a gun, and he wasn't drunk as far as I could tell, yet Del was clearly pissed. I was certainly an inviting target as I made my way through the rows of vehicles. Easy enough for a high-powered rifle. I kept walking. I reached my car; the door handle was burning hot. I looked back. Del was nowhere to be seen.

In front of the café, I noticed the door of the gray car down the street open the rest of the way. A male figure stepped out. The talking stopped, and all heads turned down the hill as the mysterious figure slowly emerged from the car. He had on a pair of aviator sunglasses, and his blond hair was combed up and back. It was the man I had first met some 20 years ago, in Maryville. Older and a little heavier, but the same man. He wore a goatee and gold chain. He had on white pants and a salmon-and-white shirt. He cut quite a figure. It was Ken McElroy's lost son, Jeffrey.

I relaxed. The others standing at the rail did not. I had told them McElroy's second-oldest son might be joining us today, but I wasn't sure they took me seriously, and if he did show up I think they were a little concerned about what he would be like. Many McElroys still lived in the area—both siblings and children—but most of them had steered a path far away from Skidmore itself after the killing. The youngest of Ken McElroy's siblings, Tim, a gentle man and avid coon hunter like his brother, worked in a pizza parlor in a small town not far from Skidmore. He still lived in the house a couple of hundred yards down the road from the house where Ken and his women and children had lived. He never came into Skidmore—or even drove through it—as far as the locals knew. It was Tim whom the banker called the morning of the shooting; it was Tim who came to the bank to get Trena and take her back to the McElroy home. It was Tim who had to tell Mabel, the elderly matriarch of the family, that her son, Ken, was dead.

"Hey, Jeff," I called out to the figure standing by the car door. He took a couple steps toward me, and said my name. The passenger's door opened, and out stepped a young black woman. As far as I knew, a black person had not lived in Skidmore for a long, long time. In my book, I had written of the 1930 lynching of a black man named Ray Gunn in Maryville, about fourteen miles from Skidmore Accused of raping a white woman, he was

14

spread-eagled on a schoolhouse roof in Maryville and set on fire, while authorities looked the other way. I had spoken to a man who had witnessed the burning as a child, standing at his father's side.

So now, it was the college educated son of Ken McElroy coming into town on the 30th anniversary of his father's murder, accompanied by a young, attractive black woman. It was hard to imagine a stranger scene.

Jeff took off his glasses. I was struck, as I was every time I saw him, by the coldness of his eyes, and how, smile or laugh as he might, they never softened. When you talked with him, you were held in the gaze, like a bug stuck to a board. For years I had heard friends and foes alike of Ken McElroy tell about the look in the man's eyes; how he could scare you to death saying nothing at all, how he could clear out a pool hall with a glance. I had not seen it in his other children, but I saw it in Jeff. It was as close to Ken McElroy as I was ever going to get. The others behind me stirred: They saw it, too. Jeff smiled, and we shook hands. He introduced me to his companion, and we walked over to meet the others.

Del Clement as a cowboy in a school play his senior year.

Del Clement, widely believed to be the primary shooter, as an auctioneer. Despite eyewitness identification, Clement was never charged. He died Jan. 9, 2009.

CHAPTER 4

I first met Jeff not too long after "In Broad Daylight" was published. He called me one night, and said that he thought he was the son of Ken McElroy and a woman I had called "Sally" in the book. Sally had been one of McElroy's first victims. A girl from a poor, rural family, McElroy had begun having sex with her when she was barely fourteen. The rumor was that he had drowned her father in a bathtub when he objected to what McElroy was doing to his daughter. Within a few years, Sally had had four children by him. It had been perhaps the local populace's first lesson in McElroy's immunity from the law.

I had not found Sally while researching the book, but I had talked to her social worker and a few others who knew her and the story. One of them recalled McElroy visiting her in the hospital after the last baby was born. At 18, she was unable to care for her four children. The social workers, nurses, and family members all recommended that she give the children up for adoption, which she finally did. As I learned later, two of the children, a boy and a girl, were adopted together, to a family in Kansas City. The boy, Jeffrey, had a hernia.

The man on the phone said his name was Jeffrey. He had read the book and put some pieces together and had come to believe he was McElroy's son with the hernia. There were a few facts I hadn't put in the book, and Jeff's knowledge matched up with them. He told me that years

17

earlier his sister, adopted by the same family in Kansas City, had found a collection of magazines and articles in a dresser drawer in their adoptive parents' bedroom, all of which led with the story of the killing of Ken Rex McElroy.

Jeff investigated and found some documents showing the date and place of his birth, which further heightened his suspicions. And there the matter lay, until he read the book. It all fit. He managed to obtain his medical records from a hospital where he had had his hernia repaired as a child. In black and white, on paper, were the names of his parents: "Ken Rex McElroy and 'Sally'. . . " He told his sister, and the two of them began the process of accepting the fact of who their father was.

Jeff had told me on the phone back then that he lived in Kansas City, and was in college, majoring in special education. After a moment of shock, I marveled at the irony: Ken McElroy, barely literate, who hadn't gone beyond the sixth grade, an outlaw who bore a special grudge toward the educated class, had fathered a son who was not only in college but was learning to teach handicapped children. Jeff and I agreed to meet on my next trip to Kansas City.

A week or so later, I received a call around 2 a.m. from a quite distraught and drunken woman who claimed that she was "Sally" in the book. She was really pissed off at me: I had said that she didn't love her kids and had left them behind, when in fact she had had no choice; she had been coerced by the social workers and nurses into giving the kids up. She had missed them every day of her life. And, she said, I didn't know the half of who Ken McElroy was or what he had done. He was much worse, more terrible than I could ever imagine. I listened, tried to pry more details from her about McElroy's conduct, but she could only keep repeating how much she loved her kids.

"Well," I finally said, "I spoke with one of your sons, just a few weeks ago. If you would like, I'll call and ask if he's willing to speak to you." She fell silent, and after a moment or two, said, "Please, please."

When I called Jeff and told him the story, he agreed to talk to his mother and asked for her number. He ended up becoming quite involved in her life, even moving out to California to live with her and try to pull her out of a long alcoholic spiral. He met one of his other two sibling. His sister from Kansas City wanted nothing to do with her mother or her other siblings. What played out between Jeff and his mother and siblings is another story, but suffice it to say that Jeff returned to Kansas City and no longer has contact with any of them.

Jeff and I lost touch over the years. When the 25th anniversary edition of "In Broad Daylight" was released in early 2007, I received another call from him. We talked and agreed to meet on my next trip to Missouri in a few months.

I came back to Missouri often—at least every other year —although there had been times in the midst of researching other books when several years passed without a visit. I felt a great affection for Skidmore and for the people who lived there. In the heart of my research, from 1982 to 1986, I had spent more time in northwest Missouri than in my home state of Colorado.

I lived with the Goslees, a highly respected farm family in Nodaway County. Q, the patriarch, and his wife, Margaret, took me into their home. I had my own bedroom at the top of the stairs, my own seat at the dinner table, and my own parking spot under the walnut tree in the drive alongside the house. Through them, I gained a respectability that set me apart from the other journalists and authors who had come to town in search of the story of Ken McElroy. Not to say that I didn't still have doors slammed in my face, and I encountered some pretty scary situations (which I will talk about later), but being, in effect, a member of the Goslee family gave me an anchor in the community.

As in all small towns, everyone knew everything about everyone else, and Q and Margaret would sit at the table after dinner and outline the genealogy of the various players in the drama. I took notes and made long lists of people to talk to. Sometimes Margaret or Q or one of their sons would call a person and lay the groundwork for my visit. An introduction from a respected local was worth its weight in gold.

When I came to town in 1983, Ken McElroy's killers were at large. The prosecuting attorney of Nodaway County, David Baird, swore that if credible evidence came to his office pointing to the identity of the killers he would prosecute them. Law officers in the area claimed that they followed up any leads that came their way. How serious Baird or law enforcement really was is open to serious question.

It was the law, after all, that time after time had failed to protect the residents of Skidmore. It was the law that, through its idleness, its willingness to be intimidated by one man, had allowed a series of events to get rolling that eventually resulted in the murder of Ken McElroy on the main street of Skidmore. It was the prosecutor after all who, after successfully prosecuting McElroy for shooting the grocer, had agreed to a continuance of the hearing to revoke his bond on the morning of his death.

When I raised the question of prosecuting the killers, the locals' anger flared: "Where the hell was the law when McElroy was running loose?" There was a compelling logic to their attitude: If the law had handled McElroy, he would not have been shot to death. But it hadn't, and he had been, and now you wanted to put in jail the men who had acted to protect the community the law had failed so terribly? You couldn't call that justice.

Not that the townspeople were particularly pleased with the killing. One attitude toward the killers I heard frequently was: "They should be given a medal for what they did, and be strung up for the way they did it." Meaning in broad daylight, at ten o'clock on a Friday morning, on the main street of town, in front of 45 witnesses. The killers didn't know it, of course, but that morning the national press was ninety miles south in Kansas City, covering the collapse of the Hyatt Hotel bridge. Nothing suited their eastern journalistic instincts more than to drive up to a small town in northwest Missouri to cover an Old West–style "vigilante killing of a town bully." The New York Times led the pack.

I had always found the fact that McElroy lived as long as he did—he was forty-seven when he was killed—to be very interesting. The young men in the area shrugged their shoulders when I asked them about it. Perhaps each one was waiting for another to take care of him. Perhaps they were scared of what would happen if they only wounded McElroy, or missed him altogether. Or maybe they were scared of going to jail, or maybe they didn't want to live with murder on their conscience, no matter how justified.

Not that a few of them hadn't thought about killing him, even planned a bit. As I mentioned in the book, one local farmer diagrammed on a napkin for me how McElroy could have been taken care: two men would wait crouched behind a clump of bushes right at the corner where the Valley Road met Route V. They would hit him with a high-powered slug as he slowed to make the turn onto the Valley on his way home. Two shooters. One would be sure to hit him. They would roll his truck into the ditch and let him lie there. He wouldn't be found until morning.

The fact is, if he had been killed this way very little would have come of it. There would have had a cursory investigation by lawmen who knew him only too well and would be relieved at his death.

Another fact is that if McElroy had been shot to death in the dark of night like that, at the intersection of V and Valley Road, there would have been no story, not for Sixty Minutes, not for Playboy, not for Rolling Stone, and not for me. There would have been no book and no movie entitled In Broad Daylight.

I once estimated that Ken McElroy had more than 20 children, by at least five women; the kids I had talked to were tremendously loyal to him. He might have beaten their mothers terribly, but he was nice to his kids. Several of them even joined me on "Oprah" and tried to explain, without much success, what a good man their father really was.

The man walking toward me now was in his early twenties when he learned who his father was. I had been somewhat apprehensive when I first met Jeff. More and more research supports the notion that in some people genetics is linked to criminal behavior. Would he be struggling with that possibility? I wondered. Would he be angry at the source of the new information about who he was? I had instead found him to be a gentle bear, in spite of the cold glare in his eyes. As we approached the railing where the others were standing, I heard a whistle, and a low-spoken muttered comment or two as those in the crowd recognized the unmistakable visage of the man who had held the town hostage for so many years.

CHAPTER 5

I was 39 when Ken McElroy died. I came across a short piece about the killing in Time Magazine. It had the famous picture of him holding a daughter in his lap and staring malevolently into the camera. I looked at the photo for several minutes, then cut it out.

As I mentioned, I had always wanted to be a writer, and over the years I told myself that someday I would be one. But what would I write about? I had long been an admirer of Truman Capote and his great work "In Cold Blood," but I hadn't written anything creative since college, when I had a short story published in the college literary magazine. Legal writing is not creative; it's the opposite of creative. Logical, linear, meant not to entertain but rather to convince. I didn't want to write newspaper stories, or even magazine articles. I wanted to write a book. But how did one go about writing a book? How did one get published? What made me think I could do it?

I read everything that was written on the killing— magazine stories, one book, and many columns. I watched Morley Safer recount the story on Sixty Minutes. All of the stories hit the easy dramatic points: the bully who got away with crimes for 20 years, the town that took the law into its own hands, and the failure of even one of the 45 or so witnesses to the killing to talk. Some stories were more wildly dramatic than others—one AP story, reprinted around the country was particularly egregious; the Rolling

Stone and Playboy pieces weren't much better. They all seemed to have one thing in common: very, very few facts.

The articles consisted mainly of rumors, hearsay, and speculation about what McElroy had done, about how he was killed, and the nature of the silence afterward. The book "Judgment Day" was terrible; it read like it had been knocked out in two weeks, relying mainly on the published accounts and the uneducated impressions of the two authors. The reason for this paucity of facts was not a mystery. No one in the town would talk. The killers were still at large and, by all accounts, still in the town's midst. FBI agents had been all over the countryside for a year, questioning and intimidating people. Trena had sued the town, and her lawyer's investigators had been on the prowl. The people were scared, and they were angry. Outsiders would be a lot less than welcome.

I understood this in part because I had lived a few years of my childhood in a small ranching town in the Sand Hills of Nebraska. Bassett consisted of 1,200 people; Skidmore had around 450. Even without two killers in their midst it would be hard to get small-town people to open up to strangers. I had no idea how I would get the story where others had failed, what I could say that would convince the locals to talk to me. I was not the sort that took rejection well, and I could only imagine the open hostility that awaited another outsider asking questions about Ken McElroy.

So I stayed where I was, in Denver. I watched as the county and state grand juries met, took testimony, and disbanded without issuing any indictments. Then, a few months later, I read that a federal grand jury had convened in Kansas City to investigate the killing. I knew from my practice that federal grand juries are powerful instruments of the law; they have the resources of the entire federal government, including assistant US attorneys and FBI

agents, at their disposal. Federal prosecutors use them
routinely to crack open crimes by turning one person
against another, by immunizing witnesses and forcing them
to talk. They had even broken omertà, the code of silence
of the Italian mob, as well as the veil of secrecy of the Ku
Klux Klan.

When several months later I read an article that the
federal grand jury had disbanded without taking action, I
was stunned. I simply could not believe that the federal
government had not been able to break down one of the
45 or so witnesses.

That did it. I either got off my butt and drove to that
small town and knocked on some doors or I quit telling
myself that one day I would write a book. I looked up
Skidmore on the map and plotted my route. I would stop
in Lincoln on the way to visit my parents, and then cross
the Missouri River and venture into the northwestern part
of the state, McElroy country. Still, I put the trip off. What
was I going to do when I got there? What was I going to
say? Where was I going to stay?

A few months later I woke up in the middle of the
night and stared into the darkness. I had crossed some line,
the point where going to Missouri and failing was
preferable to living with the feeling of not having had the
guts to even make the effort. I packed a suitcase, stuffed
notepads, pens, and a tape recorder in my briefcase, bid
good-bye to my still-sleeping wife, fed my dog and cat, and
headed east out of town, just in time to catch the sun
climbing over the eastern horizon.

CHAPTER 6

Jeff was very nervous about coming up to Skidmore, he would later tell me. He had trouble sleeping the night before the commemoration, and woke up nauseous. He considered not coming. But he was here because he wanted to know more about his past, the town, his father. Himself.

I introduced Jeff to the group standing in front of the café. He looked each person in the eye as he shook their hand. Finally, someone asked him what his involvement with the story was. He said he was "the lost son of Ken McElroy," a phrase I had used in writing about him in my blog. What could have been a difficult moment passed. People began politely asking Jeff questions about his past. Then they began telling stories about McElroy. Dunbar told the story about McElroy dumping cash on the counter in the tavern and insisting that others pick up whatever they wanted. Kirby Goslee said he had gone to high school with Jeff's mother. He told about riding the bus to school with her. On the way home after school, McElroy's truck would pull up behind the bus, the bus would pull over, and Sally would get out and get into the truck. Day after day. She couldn't have been more than 13 or 14 at the time.

Jeff kept his sunglasses off, although by now the sun was quite bright, as if to make clear that he had nothing to hide. With considerable drama, Dunbar told the story of McElroy and Trena pulling shotguns on him outside the tavern across the street. Jeff listened intently to the stories, but didn't ask any questions. The female friend at his side had kept her sunglasses on and remained quiet.

Pickups began slowing in front of the café. Heads turned in our direction. Eyes lingered on Jeff. It made me think of the stories I had heard about the main street in the hour or so after the shooting. Those on the street scattered. Many got in their trucks and left town, only to return a short time later and drive slowly past the Silverado and stare through the shattered rear window at the bulky form still slumped on the front seat, as if to convince themselves that Ken Rex McElroy was really dead.

Jeffrey Dalsing, the "lost son" of Ken McElroy, at the 30th Anniversary memorial on the main street of Skidmore, July 10, 2011. At age 19, Jeff, a college graduate, learned that Ken McElroy was his father. The resemblance is striking.

McElroy had started the truck just before he was shot. The impact of the bullets had slammed him forward and pushed his foot down on the accelerator, and the engine roared and smoked until it seized up. Some said only a minute or two. Others said 10 minutes. As word of the shooting spread, other vehicles slipped into town and drove slowly past the shot-up truck. The wife of one of the farmers on the street that morning drove six miles into town for a view, and she drove past the death scene three times before she was convinced that McElroy was dead.

I have imagined the scene over the years: After the truck shut down, the silence is deafening; not a soul on foot is about; only the trucks creep past. The sun boils hotter as the minutes pass, and McElroy lies there, alone, draining of blood, stiffening. Ten minutes. Fifteen minutes. Half an hour. An hour. No one from the town called for an ambulance or the law. God only knows how long he would have sat there before a local called it in.

The bank manager had finally phoned Tim and told him of the shooting, and Tim drove into town. He slowed behind the Silverado to see for himself what had happened to his brother. Convinced he was dead, Tim went into the bank where Trena had been sitting in a chair, crying in fear, still sure that the gunmen were coming for her. Her blonde hair sparkled with bits of glass, her blouse and jeans were splattered with blood, and a puddle had formed on the floor beneath her chair. Tim helped her out and into his truck, and they drove past the Silverado one final time. At the farm, Tim dialed the phone for Trena, who called Richard McFadin, McElroy's lawyer, who finally called the sheriff's office in Maryville to report that his client—one of his best, he always paid in cash—had been shot to death on the main street of Skidmore. Roughly an hour and a half after the shooting, an ambulance finally pulled into town and came to an abrupt stop behind the Silverado.

Jeff seemed to notice the trucks slowing, but said nothing. I wondered if the drivers thought maybe the ghost of Ken McElroy had come back to haunt them on the 30th anniversary of his death.

Since first meeting Jeff in the late eighties, I wondered how learning at age 19 or 20 that his father was Ken Rex McElroy impacted him. He told stories about how mean and abusive his adoptive parents had been, so it wasn't as if he'd had an idyllic childhood. Still it must have affected his view of himself to learn that his father was a brutal rapist, thief, arsonist, bully, and batterer. Jeff had always seemed mainly curious about it, not too worried about what it might mean about who he was, or the possibility that some monster lurked in the recesses of his soul.

When we drove up to Skidmore not too long after the book was published in 1990, and I showed him where his father had been parked when he was shot, he seemed interested in the facts, but not overly so. In fact, he seemed distanced from it, as if he were a bystander in his own life. Or it could simply have been that he knew who he was, and was comfortable with it. Certainly, in talking with him, if you could get past the look in his eyes, you felt nothing lurking, no subtle vibrations that hinted of an antisocial personality. The only connection I heard him make between himself and his father was when he wondered aloud if the fact that he had never married or had children might have something to do with it.

I had warned Jeff that if he came up here to Skidmore on the 30th anniversary of his father's death, he would be forever revealed to the world as Ken McElroy's son. I wondered for a moment if in fact in a very small way he might be reveling in it, the attention, and the new reputation it would provide. He answered each and every question forthrightly and without hesitation, in the presence of the newspaperman scribbling notes. No, I decided, he was neither scared of what might run in his blood nor taken with how the world might see him now.

In Jeff's case, the eyes were not the window to the soul; they were mainly an inherited physical characteristic, like the bulky shoulders or the thick hair. Now, Juarez, Ken's son by Alice Woods, he had the same look in his eyes, but there was an extra something in them, a meanness. Unlike Jeff, he had gone at least partway down his father's path, ending up in prison for assault. I had seen his booking picture. Richard McFadin, the lawyer who got McElroy out of trouble time and again over 20 years, had defended Juarez unsuccessfully on several assault charges.

I kept an eye out for Cheryl Brown. It was Cheryl's mother, Lois Bowenkamp, who had set off the final firestorm by refusing McElroy service after he and Trena entered the store in a fury over an employee who had supposedly accused one of McElroy's daughters of trying to steal some candy. After months of terrorizing Lois and her husband, McElroy shot Bo, Cheryl's stepfather, in the neck with a shotgun on the loading dock behind the store. At the moment McElroy was shot, Cheryl had been looking out the rear window of the store, but she always claimed she hadn't seen the shooters.

In each book, there is at least one person who steps forward and for whatever reason becomes an ally in your cause. Cheryl was one of those people. One night, at a dance in the D & G Tavern at which, ironically, the Clement Brothers Band was playing, Kermit Goslee took it upon himself to introduce me to her. She looked me up and down, and finally said, "Well, it's about time."

CHAPTER 7

The first day I drove into Skidmore all those years ago played back in my mind like a scene from a black-and-white movie. I had stayed in a motel in Maryville, and in the morning, after a long breakfast and several slow circles around the town square, I headed out over Route V to Skidmore. The road rose and fell and twisted and turned like a crazy roller coaster. I held on to the wheel and tried to think of what I was going to do when I got to town. Finally, I came to the edge of town; the fields of corn and beans grew up to the lawn of a large two-story clapboard house, which I would later learn was the home of Bo and Lois Bowenkamp.

"Skidmore, pop. 450" the road sign said, and I had a feeling that I was heading into the twilight zone. This was the town that had taken the law into its own hands, shot to death the town bully, and withdrawn behind an impenetrable curtain.

I slowed as I passed blocks of well-kept residences, noting the street names. I came to the crest of the hill, and spotted the old railway station at the bottom of it. Going up the other side was the one-block business district. Pickups were scattered on both sides of the street at odd angles. A post office was on the right. I recognized the D & G Tavern from the photos, and Mom's Café, on the left. I parked down from the café, at the end of a row of pickups. I sat there for several minutes, trying to think of what to do or say once I went in.

I finally pushed open the car door and stepped out into the heat. The curb was broken. Grass grew through the cracks in the sidewalk. The steps to the café sat at an angle. The screen door opened easily, and suddenly I was inside. In front of me were three tables, each one with three or four men seated at it, wearing jeans, shirts, work boots, and seed-dealer caps or cowboy hats. All eyes turned to me, and the hum of voices that had greeted me as I entered switched off. The slam of the screen door behind me sounded like the crack of a high-powered rifle. I stepped on in, and found a seat at the counter. The eyes looked away from me. When the waitress finally came over, I ordered coffee. It was weak and lukewarm. Chairs scraped, and several men stood, mumbled something, and walked out. I thought of following them out and approaching one of them on the street, but I stayed rooted on the stool.

After ten minutes or so, I put a few dollars next to the check on the counter in front of me, and walked out. As I hit the first step, I heard the voices inside pick up, seemingly right where they had left off when I walked in. I glanced up the street. Around the corner was the B & B Grocery, which I knew Bo and Lois still owned. I walked up, past the D & G Tavern, past the very spot where McElroy had been sitting when he was shot, past the spot where the shooters had been standing, and, despite the heat, felt a shiver run up my neck.

Lois was standing behind the counter when I walked in. Short, stocky, with brown hair and glasses, she glared at me.

"Good morning," I said, as pleasantly as I could manage.

"If you say so," she said. I walked the dim aisles, picked up a tube of toothpaste and a plastic comb. I spotted Bo working behind the meat counter in the back of the store.

I said hello to him, and he croaked something back. I caught a glimpse of the scarred tissue on his neck from the blast of McElroy's shotgun. I put the items down in front of Lois, hoping, as a customer, to earn at least a glimmer of warmth.

"That all?" she said.

I nodded, and laid out a few dollars. She tossed the items in a sack, and handed back the change. Every reporter and investigator probably did the same thing, I thought. A few cents won't buy off that attitude.

"Thanks," I said.

"Yep," she responded, and turned away.

Jesus, I thought, out on the sidewalk. That's how it's going to go. I stood on the corner by the bank and watched a few people go into the post office across the street. The postmaster would have had a perfect view of the shooting from the window, I thought. He's a federal employee. I could talk to him. I spotted a pickup stopped behind my car. The driver was staring at the Colorado plates. It moved on slowly. Time to go, I thought. I felt my feet push into the toes of my shoes as I walked down the hill, sack in hand. There wasn't a vehicle parked within five spaces on either side of my car, as if it had some sort of disease. I climbed in, backed out into the street, and headed back toward Maryville.

My guess was that Cheryl wouldn't make the commemoration. She wasn't Cheryl Brown anymore; she had been married and divorced twice since the shooting. Both Bo and her mother were dead. She and another woman used to organize and put on the yearly Punkin' Show pretty much by themselves. For a few years after the shooting, the annual celebration didn't happen, then Cheryl got it going again. She would always say how much she loved Skidmore.

I remembered watching my first Punkin' Show parade.

Greg Clement was the parade marshal, and Del was one of the judges at the tractor pull that afternoon. Gary Dowling, often mentioned as the man on the shotgun, drank and carried on loudly in the tavern as the band played country music. From the outside, it looked like any other small town, except perhaps it seemed a little too intent on having a good time.

There hadn't been a Punkin' Show in recent years. Cheryl, it seemed, had finally given up on it. The town had given up on itself. After the murder of the Stinnet girl, the past seemed to have become too much for it to bear. The patriarchs of the older generation, like Q Goslee and Pete Ward, the WWII vet who had finally stood up to McElroy, had passed away. Farms were split up. Kids moved on. The place felt like it was in an irreversible downhill slide, and no one seemed to care.

The economy had hit Skidmore hard. More people did their shopping in Maryville, where a giant Walmart had located. The B & B Grocery had long since closed. The bank at the top of the hill now served as the town hall. Mom's Café was the community center. Both gas stations had closed, although Sumy's had reopened as a tire and car repair place. The post office moved to a new building down the road, but it probably wouldn't be around for long. Houses in the neighborhood north of the main street were falling down. An outsider had, for some inexplicable reason, bought up a number of houses and stored old machinery and battered appliances in their yards. Many of the houses were rented by workers on the pipeline or employees of the plants in Maryville. There was little sense of community. Standing in front of the tavern, or in the street, you could now talk about McElroy without fear.

I had finally gotten a break. A friend of my brother Mike had gone to school with the wife of a liquor-store owner who lived in Maryville. The owner, known as JB, didn't know much more than rumors he'd heard about the shooting, but he had a close friend, a farmer, who lived in Skidmore and had been in town the day of the shooting. His name was Q Goslee, and he was third-generation farmer on the land.

The farmhouse, with a string of white outbuildings behind it, sat on top of a hill on Route V as you approached Skidmore from the south. I rang the bell by the back door, and a white-haired man with ice blue eyes came to the door. I gave his friend's name, said why I was there, and he invited me to sit with him on the porch. Q was a man of few words, but he told me what he knew about Ken and the killing. He had been in the tavern with his son Kermit on the morning of the shooting, but they hadn't followed McElroy outside. He also had a son, Kriss, who has been working on a book on the killing. He had collected lots of interviews from people involved, but he wasn't a writer. I should talk to him.

Kriss would turn out to be a mixed blessing. He was observant, insightful, smart, and articulate. He knew the town; he knew people's secrets, their affairs; he knew the underworld of Ken McElroy and his friends. But Kriss could also be quite scary. He was big-boned and loud, and exhibited a crazy sort of energy. When he drank and did drugs, he was very intimidating. He was known as a mean fighter because of an incident in which he broke a man's arm by laying it across a curb and stomping on it. Some locals even referred to him as a junior McElroy. Although he wasn't in town the morning of the shooting, he knew what had happened in the killing of Ken McElroy. He had taped a lot of interviews, but I came to suspect that some of the people talked to him because it was easier than refusing him. On the day I met him, he proudly showed me a plastic bag full of pieces of McElroy's skull that he had obtained from a man who had collected them from the dash of the Silverado.

Once Kriss and I reached an arrangement, he turned over the transcription of the tapes to me, and we began making a long list of people to be interviewed. I returned home, got my life organized, and drove back to Skidmore, now with a plan of sorts.

The Goslees invited me to move into the house. Margaret set a place for me at the table and did my laundry. Kirby, the brother who farmed the land with Q, took to the idea of the book immediately. On my first day there, he called up the mayor, who had been on the street and witnessed the shooting, and asked him to talk to me. Kermit, an auctioneer who also sold real estate, was a little more hesitant, but eventually we became good friends. In the beginning, Q wasn't quite as supportive.

It reminded me of the anthropologist Margaret Mead, who when studying tribal societies, befriended the highly respected elders in the tribe. This connection not only gave me a base, it gave me a certain level of respectability.

CHAPTER 8

Standing in front of the café, I felt a light wind arise. It reminded me how terrible the wind could be in Missouri. It blew strong, or it blew in gusts, but by noon it was almost always blowing. In the winter it was laced with ice, and often dropped the temperature below zero. The Goslee farmhouse stood on top of a hill, and sometimes it blew so cold up there you could almost freeze on the way from the car to the house. In the summer it swirled the hot, wet air like a blast furnace.

I would come to spend many days scouring the back roads of northwest Missouri, tracking down lawmen, witnesses, jurors, and prosecutors, as well as friends, family, victims, and enemies of Ken McElroy. My Mazda had no air-conditioning, so in the summer I could either leave the windows closed and let the car boil, or open them to the hot wind. Most back roads weren't marked thirty years ago, and locals talked in terms of directions: "Go west three miles, and you'll see the house on the north side of the road, where you turn east. . . ." I always tried—usually with little success—to get the locals to translate it into "lefts" and "rights."

I often parked down the road from my quarry's house to prepare myself for the encounter. I practiced my opening line, and thought of follow-up questions. I lay my head back on the headrest, and tried to calm the flutter in my stomach. Most of these folks didn't appreciate strangers anyway, much less ones who were poking around the killing of Ken McElroy.

One day, I went searching for one of McElroy's older sisters who lived out in the country. I found the farm, and spotted an elderly man on a tractor in a field next to the house. I parked and waved to him. He stopped, and turned off the tractor. At least in his mid-80s, he was startlingly skeletal. He had one good eye and an empty socket in the other, and both seemed to be staring at me. I yelled across the ditch to him that I was doing some research on the killing of Ken McElroy and would like to talk to him. He said something I couldn't hear, and I stepped across the ditch and up to the barbed wire fence. He said there wasn't "no use in talking about it," but Ken wasn't as bad as they said, and the people in Skidmore didn't think about what it did to his brothers and sisters, his kids, when they killed him. Pleased to at least have him talking, I asked him about his wife, the sister, and what the killing had done to her. At the mention of her name, he paused, glared at me with his ghostly face, and told me he had nothing more to say.

"What is it, Carl?" a female voice called from the farmhouse.

"Got a guy here asking about Ken." I heard the door slam. "You best be getting," he said. "She'll be bringing the shotgun."

In the beginning, I had a few doors shut in my face, some with a little speech, others silently. The common attitude was that the whole McElroy thing was in the past and that's where it should be left. Let sleeping dogs lie. If the person came out onto the porch, or even just opened the door all the way, I at least had a chance to make my pitch. Notebook in hand, I would explain that I was a writer from Colorado, and that I was trying to get the facts of the story right, as opposed to all the junk in the papers and TV.

I got smarter as I went along. I learned to spin my story depending on whom I talked to. To a family member I would say that I wanted to tell Ken's side of the story; to a victim I would say I wanted to get the complete story of just how terrible it had been. To town residents, I would say how awful it was that the criminal justice system had let them down, stressing that as a lawyer I would be able to lay out its screw-ups, chapter and verse. "Ken had a lot of friends, I know that," I would say to a girlfriend or offspring. To one of the jurors who had voted to acquit McElroy of shooting Romaine Henry in the stomach, I would assure him that it couldn't have been an easy task sitting in judgment on a man like McElroy.

There had been a witness to McElroy's vicious assault on Romaine Henry, but he had conveniently disappeared the week before trial. I found the young man in a house in the woods outside a nearby town, and he was still scared to death, even though by then McElroy had been dead for two years. I promised I would not reveal his name or identify him in any way, if he would just tell me what he saw. He could only manage a few phrases before he disappeared behind the door.

Women were, not unexpectedly, generally less inclined to behave rudely when approached. I tried to be as pleasant as I could, and stress that I was trying to be fair, but that I really needed some assistance. I wouldn't be much of a bother, if she could just explain a thing or two. Often I would be invited in and offered a seat at the kitchen table and something to drink. I talked about the weather, farming, TV shows, before gradually coming around to Skidmore and McElroy, usually with a broad question, such as what did she make of it all. I let her define the direction of the conversation from there, gently nudging the flow now and then.

One woman who had gone through grade school with

McElroy brought out her sixth grade class picture. I was startled by the good looks of the tall, lanky fellow in the back row. (McElroy had been held back two grades). I lay the photo casually on the table in front of me. Only as I was rising to leave, after two hours, when goodwill had been clearly established, did I casually ask if I could take the picture and have it copied. She assented easily.

I came to understand quite clearly one thing about human nature: No one, and I mean no one, in this world thinks they are listened to enough. I learned the art of listening, and I became quite good at it. You put the interviewee on center stage, and it was only what he or she had to say that mattered. My thoughts and perceptions and stories were of no concern. How often does that happen in life? I would nod my head, or shake it as the case might be, and follow up with a question that clearly demonstrated I was not only listening but was genuinely interested in what the person had to say. Occasionally, the person would catch himself, and only then would I try to distract him by telling a story about myself or my struggles here in Nodaway County. I would leave the porch or living room when there was still a little more to tell, so I could ask if I might return. Yes, the person would almost always say. What a polite fellow.

I learned to keep my notebook in my back pocket. Only when the subject was talking and had reached a certain level of comfort with my presence would I interrupt gently, reach into my back pocket, and ask, "Would you mind if I took notes? I'm afraid I won't remember it all." Usually there was just a nod, and the story would continue.

On a second interview, I would say, "I would rather just listen and not have to struggle to write everything down. Would you mind if I taped it?" Some refused, but most nodded. They would stare at the recorder on the table in front of them for a few moments, and then continue on as if it weren't there.

A lot of the locals felt that the national press had treated them terribly unfairly, referring to them as "vigilantes," or twisting their quotes into something that they didn't say, making them look like a bunch of ignorant, violent hicks. They particularly resented the writer from Playboy, who had come to town in his pressed jeans and a pint of Jack in his back pocket, and with a snotty New Jersey attitude. It amused them that he had been so nervous about the place that he stayed in a hotel 40 miles south in St. Joe.

I always told a person, if I had the chance, that I had grown up in a small town in Nebraska, much like Skidmore, and I understood their way of life and respected their desire for privacy. But it was important to get the town's story right, I would insist. I wanted to know what it was like living in Skidmore under McElroy's reign of terror. I promised to search the courthouse records and detail how he flaunted the law and got away with everything year after year.

I also made one point clear to everyone I spoke with: I was not trying to solve the killing; I wasn't going to unmask the killers in the book. It really didn't make much difference who shot McElroy that morning, I would insist, because someone else would have done it the next day, or the day after that. Not only did this put them at some ease, but early on I came to believe that I already knew who had killed McElroy and how it all went down. I had heard the story two or three times without asking. Which in fact caused me some concern. I would get occasional veiled warnings: Someone would say he didn't think it was a good idea for me to be asking so many questions, or another that he had heard that I was stirring things up that should be left alone. The one thing that worried me the most was that someone would repeat the fact that he had told me what had happened on the street that day, and that would get back to the killers themselves.

As time went on, I got to know the locals by the trucks they drove. One night, after I had been around for about six months, I came out of the tavern, where a dance was going on, to find Del Clement's truck, with a horse trailer attached, blocking my car. I went back inside and mentioned it to Kermit Goslee, who said to do nothing. I went out after midnight, and the truck was gone. I took it as a warning. Another night I came out of the tavern to see a man crouched by the rear tire of my car with something in his hand. He fled when he saw me. On the tire was the beginning of a slash mark. Another five seconds and the deed would have been done.

CHAPTER 9

Right about now, a few minutes after ten o'clock, I figured McElroy would have been walking out of the tavern, holding a brown sack containing a six-pack and a pack of cigarettes. There had been at least 25 men in the tavern, and some said things to his back probably no man had said to Ken McElroy in his life. Trena had whispered something about leaving, and he had shrugged her off. Then he stood, looked around, grabbed the sack, and walked out. He was either egging them on, drawing them outside, or he was trying to get out before the thing came apart. I've never made up my mind which, although I tend to go with the former.

McElroy was 47 years old and had gotten heavy. His two favorite pastimes, hunting coon and having sex with young women, were becoming harder and harder for him to engage in. He couldn't run through the fields after his dogs anymore. He no longer cut the striking figure that put girls off their guard. Most likely, unless McFadin could pull off a miracle, he was on his way to prison. McElroy probably figured that none of the men in there, with the exception of Pete Ward, had the guts to face him down. Perhaps he thought twice about the men behind the bar, Del and Gregg Clement. Del was there when he came in, and he had been drinking beer steadily. Del was known as a drunk and a hothead, and he always kept a loaded rifle in his truck. McElroy had come to town unarmed.

Maybe McElroy kept track of the men in the tavern and figured he would get after them one by one when things cooled down. Maybe he wanted to call their bluff, see if they really had the guts to shoot him. He must have seen the others, standing in the street outside, waiting. It would be 50 to one. If he called their bluff, if he drove out of town this morning alive, he would own the place.

Trena followed him out the door, like always. Then 15 or 20 of the onlookers went through the door to watch him leave, to stare him down—let him know the old days were over. Several of them walked a few yards up the street, a few stood in the middle of the street, and others stopped not far from the bed of his truck. The men at Sumy's station watched the scene from on top of the hill. McElroy probably didn't notice the figure in the white cowboy hat walk quickly out the back door of the tavern and across the street to his truck. McElroy settled into the Silverado, started it, and opened the pack of cigarettes.

"Shoot the sonofabitch!" someone shouted.

Trena turned around in time to see the cowboy pull a high-powered rifle from the rack in his truck, snap a shell into the chamber, and raise it to his shoulder. She called to Ken that they were going to shoot him. If he had believed her, Ken could have ducked out of sight, or stepped out of the truck to make them look him in the eye, or started backing up into them. Instead, he flicked open the lighter and lit a cigarette, convinced that they didn't have the guts to do it or, perhaps, almost wishing they did. The cigarette ended up splattered on the dashboard, the lighter on the floor.

The writer from the Maryville paper asked Jeff a lot of questions about his past, where he lived and where he worked. Jeff answered the questions calmly, almost matter-of-factly, only a slight nervousness showing in his hands. Dunbar's girlfriend asked him questions about his mother, his siblings, the type of children he worked with, what it was like when he realized he was Ken's son. It got so personal at one point, I almost stepped in as a shield. The reporter took a photo of Jeff and Dunbar looking at my book.

I waited to see if Jeff would begin asking questions about the town, his father, mother, siblings—but he didn't. He answered questions politely and listened to the stories about his father and mother. The woman at his side remained silent.

A car slowed and parked up the hill from us. Out stepped Jim Hartman, the postmaster at the time of the killing, now retired. I had interviewed Jim several times, convinced he had seen what happened on the street and wanting him to set the scene for me, but he always said he was behind the counter in the back when the shooting started. He insisted that by the time he got to the front window the street was cleared. Today, he walked over, shook my hand, and said he heard I was in town and wanted to say hello. I introduced him to Jeff.

I heard that after the shooting stopped, Hartman came out of the post office—now the café—and picked up a cluster of .22 shells that had fallen on the street next to the curb. He had never admitted it. I glanced across at the tavern, down at the curb. We were standing about where the shells would have fallen.

Not that the shells would have proven much. The guns were never found. And I thought I knew why. One night, after I had been around quite a while, I was drinking by myself at the Palms, a bar in Maryville, when one of the local farmers slid in next to me at the bar and ordered a drink. He had been in town the day of the killing, and I had interviewed him, but he hadn't given me much. Early on I had learned the art of non-interviewing: talking about things that had nothing to do with McElroy or the shooting. Just hanging around in the café, or the bar, or a tractor pull, tempting others to forget who I was and why I was there. Drinking was one of the easiest ways to do it. I bought the farmer his second beer, and we talked about some new strains of seed corn he had planted. He noticed some buddies sitting at a table in the corner. Several of them had been on the street that day, and were friends of the Clements. They motioned him over. "Come on," he said, grabbing both of our beers, not thinking twice. I almost grabbed for my beer back. They had been drinking hard. Who knew how they would react to me?

The farmer set the two beers down at the table. "You guys met Harry? From Colorado?"

"Howdy," I said.

"Colorado?" one of them said. "I got a sister lives in Arvada." The others glanced at me, with how much recognition I couldn't tell. I slid in next to my friend, and started going on about how I had lived in Arvada when I first got to town, and how much it had changed in the past 20 years. Someone else said he drove through the Rockies on the way to Las Vegas and got caught in a snow slide outside of Glenwood Springs. And from there the conversation went on. They were drinking rounds of beer and shots of peach schnapps. I knew that I needed to not only buy a round when it came my turn, but I needed to drink every one of the rounds, shots included. I did, and soon I was half-drunk, tossing in comments when I could.

Worried that I would forget things, every 20 minutes or so I would excuse myself and head to the tiny closet that served as the men's room. There I would scribble notes on a deposit slip on the back of the toilet; one word for each thought, praying I could remember what the word meant when I got home. I got drunker and drunker.

Finally, someone mentioned the day of the killing. I dropped my head and began picking at the label on my beer bottle. With all the alcohol, things could easily go bad in an instant. One fellow in a seed-dealer's cap, whom I knew ranched not far from the Clements, and another guy in a cowboy hat, whom I did not know, began discussing what happened with the weapons. I gathered that not long after the shooting a call had gone out to five or six men, and they had met at a farmhouse. In the barn, the men disassembled the two rifles. One of them used an acetylene torch to cut the barrels of the two rifles into segments the size of a man's little finger. The segments were distributed among the men, and they left with the instructions to throw them down a well or into a lake or deep in the woods. Outside the barn, the men built a fire. When it blazed, they tossed the stocks in and watched them burn.

I tried to pay attention, while not looking directly at either of the speakers. The waitress, a college student, appeared. "Another round," I said quickly, motioning with my finger, "shots, too." Now thoroughly drunk, I excused myself once again to go to the bathroom— I couldn't be gone too long—and scribbled words like barrel, torch, barn, and well across the back of the slip. I stuffed it in my wallet, jammed the pen in my pants pocket, and walked out.

On my return to the table, no one paid me any mind, but even in my stupor I noticed the topic had changed to the question of when to take the crops out of the field. I drank the fresh beer and shot. Shortly after one A.M. I stumbled from the table toward the door, exhilarated, scared, and nervous as hell about driving the roller-coaster road home drunk.

CHAPTER 10

"Say, Jim," I said, "weren't you the one that picked up the shells right here next to the curb?" I pointed to the spot.

"That's what some people say," he said with a chuckle. I figured he probably picked up the shells, and did something with them. Like so many others, he must have lied to the police, the county grand jury, the state grand jury, the FBI, and the federal grand jury. Raised their hand, swore an oath to tell the truth, and lied.

"I didn't see a thing."

"I heard the shots and ducked between the cars."

Or, "I heard the shots and took off between the buildings." By the time anyone looked up, there was nothing to see. The guns were gone. The guys at Sumy's station, at the top of the street, would have been looking right at the shooters. Others a few feet uphill from them would have turned when the voice yelled out, "Shoot the sonofabitch!" and seen what was happening. There would have been no reason for them to duck or run. Anyone's first instinct would have been to look at where the shots seemed to be coming from, so as to know which way to duck or run.

Even those downhill, at the back and to the sides of the Silverado—not more than 10 or 15 yards from the shooters—would have turned to see the source of the shots, if not before they hit the ground, then the very next moment. They knew it wasn't Ken shooting. The odds are, many of them heard the shots, saw the window shatter and the head break apart, and then looked directly at the shooters. The killers would have paused for an instant, perhaps stunned by the success of their handiwork, stocks on their hips, eyes locked on the blown-apart window, the head, before they snapped back and turned to their pickups and threw the weapons inside. Every eye on the street would have seen the shooters, rifles in hand, standing there for the brief moment of conquest, celebration, before self-preservation set in. The law knew it, the men knew the law knew it, the law knew the men knew the law knew it. Everyone knew it.

Actually, I think many of the men on the street might have guessed what was likely to happen when they saw the figure in the white cowboy hat exit the back door of the tavern and walk rapidly across the street to his pickup. After all that went on in the past year—not to mention the past 20 years—someone was going to break. You might have thought it would have been Pete Ward, who had turned McElroy in for carrying a gun into the tavern, and who had seen McElroy sneaking around his house with a pistol in hand, and whom McElroy had threatened to take care of.

The last thread of civilization in that small town had snapped the morning the prosecutor had called to say that the hearing to revoke McElroy's bond, imposed after his conviction for shooting Bo, had been postponed at the request of McElroy's attorney. The men who had signed the affidavits swearing they had seen him with the gun in the tavern and heard him threaten the life of Bo might as well as have had targets painted on their backs. McElroy knew the drill: Shoot one of them, the others would quickly forget what they saw. He would soon be coming for them. With Trena riding shotgun. She might have been his victim, raped—captured really—when she was twelve, but goddamn it, she had been riding with him the last couple of years, dropping shotguns on people, firing in the air, watching McElroy's back.

After the first shots rang out, someone jerked open her door and pulled her out. She said it was Jack Clement, Del's father, and that was what I had always heard. It made sense: To kill a woman would go against the law of the Old West. Jack dragged her up the street, while, splattered in blood, she kicked and screamed.

The town's silence after the killing was, to me, as fascinating as the killing itself, or the reign of terror that had preceded it. One imagines a great conspiracy, with phone calls whipping around the countryside in the hours after the killing, brief statements traded about the need to stick together, with grunted assents. Maybe even suggesting a story about what they hadn't seen. Maybe small groups meeting at a farm or ranch to confirm how the conspiracy was holding. Perhaps this did happen among the killers themselves and a few of their closest friends, but the discussions didn't spread to the witnesses, all of the other men in the tavern or on the street that day.

Their reaction was instinctive: Keep your mouth closed. Don't tell your sons what happened, or your daughters, or your wives. Act like it never happened. Like you weren't even there. It was the way it had to be. Most of the men on the street that day drove back to their farms, after perhaps a tour or two by the truck to confirm McElroy was dead, perhaps announced to those at home that McElroy had been killed, and then got back on their tractors to spray their fields for weeds, or fixed a broken piece of machinery, or drove into Maryville for supplies. Most of them, I was convinced, never spoke of what they saw. The tribal instinct was too powerful. The guys who did the shooting might have been stupid to do what they did, the way they did it, in broad daylight, but in the end it was "us against them." "Them" was the rest of the world.

Still, there had to be a price to pay. Most of the farmers had at most a high school education. A few, like Q and Margaret and three of their sons, had gone to college. Most had not traveled too far from home; Kansas City for baseball or football games; Las Vegas to gamble; California to visit relatives; Canada to fish. Most of them grew up with a compelling work ethic. Q used to say you could tell almost all you needed to know about a man by how hard he worked. A lot of the younger ones drank hard, at the bars in Skidmore and surrounding towns. (Most stayed out of the Shady Lady in Maryville, one of McElroy's hangouts). Some went to church, but, as I mentioned, you never felt much of a religious influence in the place. The town looked out for itself, and did not turn to the government to solve its problems. Perhaps that was why so little had been done about McElroy prior to his shooting. Action was a long time coming, and when it did come it went from almost nothing to murder.

The people of Skidmore were basically honest, hardworking people. If they had any contact with the law it was for DUIs or divorces or bankruptcies. What they knew about the intricate workings of the criminal legal system they learned from TV. But they were smart enough to know that if they lied to an FBI agent, or took an oath to tell the truth in a court of law and then lied, they would be breaking a moral code as well as committing a crime. Yet, one by one they went in front of the county and state grand juries and lied about what they had seen.

When I read that a federal grand jury had been impaneled in Kansas City to investigate the killing, I had no doubt that the FBI agents assigned to the case would be able to break the silence. A good portion of their job was to get people to talk who didn't want to talk. They had an array of tried-and-true techniques: isolating, threatening, even lying to a subject. They would tell one farmer that others had talked about what they had seen, about what he had seen. He could go to jail himself. It shouldn't be hard to break one or two, or even more, of the witnesses. They only had to get one, or perhaps two, to corroborate Trena's testimony about who shot her husband. When I read an AP blurb a few months later that the grand jury had disbanded without an indictment, I simply could not believe the federal government couldn't crack one person.

I knew somewhere deep in their souls the farmers had to feel bad about lying under oath. They might not have been particularly religious, but they knew it was a sin to break an oath before God. Yet time and again they had lied. What did it do to them? I wondered. It was a question I never could fully answer.

I knew the witnesses' rationale for being untruthful. McElroy had run loose for more than 20 years. He had raped, robbed, burned, bullied, thieved, and shot people all over the county—several surrounding counties as well—with near impunity. The law didn't do its job. The law was scared of him. The system failed the people in town. And now the law sought their help in prosecuting those who solved the problem it couldn't? That was bullshit.

The witnesses said it with a certain bitterness, even anger, at being placed in the position they were in; anger at McElroy, anger at the law, and anger at the shooters. Nobody wanted to see what they had seen. Nobody wanted the law coming onto their farms, pulling them off their tractors; nobody wanted to have to lie time and again. Perhaps McElroy needed killing, but he didn't need it that way, in front of the whole world, in front of them, their eyes. But it always came back to one point: If the law had done its job, it wouldn't have come to this.

The only doubt I ever heard expressed by the locals about the righteousness of the killing was by a few women in the community. Killing was never the right way to deal with a problem. And what about his children? What would this do to them? But theirs was a small voice, and expressed to me with considerable reluctance. The cohesion of the community around the killing was strong.

Which raises another point: If one of the witnesses had identified the shooter(s) in front of a grand jury, and stuck with it, he would have been finished in Nodaway County. His ostracism, and probably that of his wife and children, would have been profound, immediate and complete. They would have had to start life over. That would be a terrible price to pay; just, as for some—not all, by any means—it was a terrible price to have seen what they saw, a terrible price to lie in the face of God.

CHAPTER 11

Jim Hartman shook my hand, and moved on. A pickup stopped in the intersection, and the driver called out my name and waved. He had been one of the kids who had been playing in the alley minutes before McElroy had shot the grocer. I called back to him. He glanced at Jeff, and drove on.

Suddenly, the scene on the street seemed to freeze. The voices fell silent. Even the wind fell still. I heard the voice ring out: "Shoot the sonofabitch!" The air split with the explosion of the .30-30: once, twice, three times. The window smashed, the broken head jerked forward. The air held the sounds of the .22 snapping and the boom of the shotgun, Trena's screaming. Then those sounds fell silent, and all you could hear was the roar of the pickup. Jesus, I thought. I glanced at my watch. Right on time. I glanced around; no one else seemed to notice anything.

Dunbar leaned forward on the iron railing and addressed Jeff. "You know, buddy, I think it takes a helluva lot of guts to come to town like this. I'm fucking impressed." The others agreed, and I could tell they meant it; they were impressed. Jeff smiled, said he had had second thoughts, but was curious. He had kept his sunglasses off in the bright sun. Now he put them on. Kirby told Jeff to get in touch if he ever came to town again. Dunbar agreed. A few phone numbers were exchanged. The reporter took a few more photos and left.

Someone gave me a book to sign. The air was heating up; the wind blew in light, short gusts. It was getting time to move on.

I was going to take Jeff and his friend on a tour of the main sites of the story. I pointed out where his father's truck had been sitting and asked Jeff to pose in front of the tavern. He stood a few feet from where his father had been killed; only a few feet from where his father had dropped a shotgun on Dunbar; only a few feet from the alley where his father had jerked the Silverado to a stop and stepped out with a shotgun in his hands; only a few feet from the loading dock at the back of the grocery where Bo had been standing and cutting up boxes.

The alley was overgrown. The paint on the back of the grocery was peeling, and it was covered with vines. The dock had fallen apart; the wooden planks were split and broken. Only the iron handrail and the steps remained intact. Bo had been an old man when McElroy shot him, tall and skinny and bald, and it made no sense. It was Lois who had refused to sell McElroy a pack of cigarettes, not Bo. Bo's only sin was that he was married to Lois. Maybe McElroy thought he saw on Bo's face the smirk of every farmer who had ever looked down on the McElroys, the poor hog farmers who lived on the edge of town; or maybe McElroy was infuriated by what he saw as Bo's weakness—his subordination to a woman. (If Bo hadn't twitched to his left at the last second, the lower half of his face and his throat and neck would have been blown away.) For McElroy, it was a stupid thing to do, shoot an unarmed man in the middle of town, and as soon as the grocer fell down on the dock, blood spurting from his neck, McElroy must have realized it. He raced home, grabbed Trena, and took off for the Missouri River and the state of Kansas.

Bo was one of the true heroes of the story. Like Romaine Henry but unlike many of McElroy's other victims, Bo had held his ground and gone to court and testified against the man who shot him. Although McElroy's claim of self-defense was laughable—he testified that Bo was coming at him with a box cutter—still, the conviction was a shock. The decision of the judge to let him out on bail was unconscionable. (The judge refused repeated requests for an interview.)

Jeff posed in front of the dock, just about where his father would have been standing when he shot Bo. He had a smile on his face, and I was struck once again about how he seemed so unaffected by the knowledge of who his father was, so unconcerned about what it might say about who he was. He must in fact be comfortable with who he is, I thought.

We got in the car. I pointed out the front of the grocery store, where McElroy bullied Lois and Bo over the shoplifting incident, and the door to the bank where Trena had been taken. I thought of driving by the Clement ranch, but I wasn't sure I could still find it. The Clements loved their horses, and I had heard stories about how McElroy would pull his pickup next to the fence bordering the field where the horses were and hang a rifle out the window pointing in the direction of the animals. Never shooting, just pointing. So far as I knew, no Clement had ever confronted him over it.

We left the place of the killing and headed out of town to the Valley Road, which would take us to the old McElroy place. It wasn't the Valley Road anymore; after 9/11 the back roads of Nodaway had all been given numbers. As we turned onto the gravel road, I recalled driving down it on one of my first trips here and stopping in at the farmhouses of a few of McElroy's neighbors, some whom had had run-ins with him. I thought they might be ready to talk about it now. One man, as soon as he heard McElroy's name, said gruffly that he had nothing to say and closed the door. He's dead!" I wanted to yell at the door, "They killed him! It's over!"

One thing I learned early on, though, was never to assume who would talk to you and who wouldn't. You knocked on every door; you wrote down every name; you called every phone number. Those who you think won't talk to you sometimes seemed almost anxious to talk. Some seemed even hurt that no one had tried to talk to them before. When I called Alice Woods, the woman who had borne three children by McElroy, I was sure I would run into a buzz saw of hostility. Instead, Alice agreed readily to an interview. We arranged a time, and she gave me explicit directions to her house in St. Joe. Over the course of the next year, I must have taped more than 20 hours of interviews with her. She talked freely about how Ken used to beat her up— smashing the stock of a shotgun into her head—but how good he was with his kids. She denied, not surprisingly, ever having participated in any of his thefts, although I had convincing evidence to the contrary.

Brian Denehey as Ken McElroy in a promo shot for the movie "In Broad Daylight."

CHAPTER 12

In Skidmore, my practice was to type up all of the interviews the same day they occurred. I would sit up in my room at the head of the stairs in the Goslee farmhouse and bang away on my portable typewriter far into the night. Every morning I sat down with Kriss, the youngest Goslee brother, and we worked on a master list of people to be interviewed, and from that we compiled a shorter list of people to try to hit that day. Kriss would give me the background on the people, where they lived, and what their connection to the story was. I gauged the success of the day's effort by how many people I could cross off the list by the end, even if all I got from someone was a door slammed in my face.

One problem was that if an interview went well, I would end up with several more names to add to the list. If it went really well, I would end up with phone numbers and directions to the people's houses. So, really, I fought a losing battle. Scratch one name off, add two.

In the early days, I had no real idea of what I was doing. I just knew I was going to tell a story, and for the story I needed facts. I came back to Skidmore month after month, year after year, talking to anyone who would talk to me. I felt like I was trudging up an endless hill, with the hope that someday I would reach the top, and I would be able to see the rest of the way clearly.

Meanwhile, I kept adding to and subtracting from the

list. Every now and then I would put together a proposal and send it off to an agent in New York. Those who bothered to reply would say something like, "It's a good story, but what makes you think you could write it?" What indeed? I had never written anything before. I pushed the question away, knowing there would come a day when I would have to face it.

I spent a lot of time in the small towns where McElroy had committed his crimes, or where he had been tried for committing his crimes, talking to victims, witnesses, jurors, judges, and prosecutors. His acquittal in the shooting of Romaine Henry was perhaps the point at which Skidmore and all of Nodaway County came to realize that there was no law and order when it came to Ken Rex McElroy. Down the road from Romaine's farm, McElroy had pulled him from his car, stuck a shotgun in his stomach, and pulled the trigger. For some reason, Romaine did not die. McFadin got the trial moved to another county, claiming that his client couldn't get a fair trial in Nodaway County because of his reputation. Romaine got on the stand and told exactly what had happened. One witness claimed to have seen McElroy's truck in the area at the time. McElroy put on a couple of ne'er-do-wells who claimed he was somewhere else at the time of the shooting. It took the jury less than hour to find McElroy not guilty.

I'd heard rumors that some jurors had found snakes in their mailboxes and others had been offered bribes for a "not guilty" vote. I wanted to talk to them. It could take me half a day to find one of them, stopping two or three times to ask directions, only to have the door closed in my face, or learn that the person had died, or lived somewhere else. A promise not to use the person's name brought little help; most could simply not imagine any good would come from talking to me. One by one, I went through the twelve jurors, scattered all over the countryside, until I found one who invited me in for iced tea. He recounted the trial and jury deliberations. As for the acquittal, he just didn't believe Romaine Henry, he said, although he couldn't explain why. The juror denied ever being threatened or offered a bribe. There was a man, though, a friend of his and McElroy's who lived farther out in the country, who said McElroy had come to him and asked him to offer the juror money to throw the verdict.

I finished my iced tea and was getting ready to close my notebook, when I asked if he thought his friend would talk to me.

"There's no saying," he said. "But he's a very big man, and if it looks like he doesn't want you around, then skedaddle the hell out of there." He looked at me hard, to impress his point. He gave the directions in the usual way: Go north two or three miles, then follow the gravel road until you come to a three-story white farmhouse, then turn west and go. . . . I scribbled in my notebook, and drew out a rough map.

I slid into the hot car, and hesitated. What was the likelihood that one of McElroy's friends was going to talk to me? I would probably spend two or three hours finding the place, and the guy would run me off, or worse. I had been around northwest Missouri long enough to know that there were people living out in the woods who barely figured as members of society. They found a way to make a meager living—driving a grain truck, raising a few hogs, shooting coons and selling their hides, buying and selling coon dogs—but they lived in the wild, at the end of twisty, rutted roads deep in the forest. They didn't vote, they didn't have bank accounts, they drank excessively, and they had lots of guns. They had a deep mistrust for strangers. These were the guys who rode with Ken McElroy, and I had to decide if I wanted to track one of them down in his den.

It was past noon on a hot, sweltering August day. The inside of my car was steaming. I had no water, and my shirt was stuck to my back. It was an hour and a half back to Maryville, and it was only going to get hotter. You never know, I reminded myself. I flattened the piece of paper on my lap, and turned off into the country.

As I proceeded farther into the countryside, making a series of turns on unmarked roads, I wondered if I should leave a trail of crumbs to find my way back out. Finally, the road turned to dirt, and eventually I turned right on a road leading through an opening in the woods. The road was a deeply rutted path, and it twisted and turned into darkness. "Fuck, fuck, fuck," I muttered. The Mazda bumped and rocked and rolled, until finally, after half a mile or so, far ahead, I could see a clearing. At the far end of the clearing was a small house. In the yard were various pieces of equipment and a pen with coon dogs. I decided to stop the car at the edge of the clearing, get out, and walk the rest of the way so whoever was inside could see that I had no gun, that even though I was a stranger, I meant them no harm.

So, I stuck my notepad in my back pocket, opened the door, and got out. I tried to walk confidently, but not threateningly, across the clearing. I could see darkness through the porch screen door. I could also see a small dog, a terrier of some sort, a few feet in front of the house, facing the door. As I got closer, I waited for him to hear me and turn. He didn't move, and didn't move. He's deaf, I thought. And I knew what was going to happen; he was going to hear me at the last second, then turn and bite me. Yet I had no choice but to keep walking. Sure enough, he heard me when I was about three feet behind him, whirled, barked, and attacked. I couldn't kick, or even curse the animal. I could only stand and take it. He latched onto my right thigh, and I could feel the teeth break the flesh through the jeans. He growled and kept biting. Finally, I heard a voice in the door. The largest man I had ever seen filled the doorway. He chuckled at the sight, and made some noise to the dog. The dog quit, and backed off. Laughing is good, I thought. Better than angry. I tried to smile in return, and reached down and pulled up my pant leg, revealing small trickles of blood from three tooth marks.

"Sorry about that," the man said, still chuckling. "The dog doesn't hear too well anymore." He was in bib overalls and T-shirt and work boots. I figured he would have to turn sideways to make it through the door, and even then it would be close.

"Come on in here, and let my wife take a look at it."

The dog bite worked in my favor in a way I could never have imagined. I was the injured stranger, but I made it clear I was not aggrieved by the attack, and I was grateful for the medical care. His wife was large too, with a full head of raven hair and pretty in an earth-mother kind of way. She apologized for the dog: "We don't get many strangers out here." She cleaned the wound, put some bandages on it, and brought me a glass of iced tea.

I expected it all to change when I said the name Ken McElroy. I couldn't have been more wrong. "Kenny" was a good friend of his, had been for many years. They had hunted coons together and traded dogs and competed at meets. Why, he and Trena used to stop by from time to time. Only a week before he was shot they had stopped by for a visit, and Trena sat at the very spot where I was sitting. Kenny came to look at a couple of his dogs; wanted to trade his blue tick for a walker or a redbone. Usually, Kenny made Trena wait outside in the truck, but today she came in with him. She usually didn't have much to say; Kenny did all the talking. My hosts always felt a little sorry for her, like she was just an attachment to Kenny.

The man talked about how McElroy was an expert with the dogs; at meets he could make $1,000 or so trading them. He was square with everyone, and no one ever fucked with him. As a friend he couldn't be a better man.

"What did you think when he was shot?" I finally asked.

He leaned forward in his chair. "I saw it on television. Said Kenny had been shot to death on the main street of Skidmore. To tell you the truth, I wasn't too surprised. He had pushed those people in Skidmore awful hard. I figured something was going to happen, sooner or later. I felt bad about it, but I understood why it happened."

I was stunned.

His Irish-looking wife nodded her head. "You can only push people so far," she said. Although killing was the wrong thing to do, she understood it. She worried about poor Trena and the kids. What did I know of them?

Finally, I got up the nerve to ask about the bribe. The man chuckled. Kenny had stopped by a few days before the trial, leaving Trena in the truck this time. "He said he was going on trial for assault. He had a piece of paper in his hand, a list, and he showed it to me, and asked if I knew any of the people on it. I pointed to one. He asked me if I would be willing to offer him a couple hundred dollars to vote 'not guilty.' I said I would, but I never did. After a few minutes he folded up the paper and left. He said he had a couple other people to visit, and he thought he might have some luck with them."

The three of us talked coon hunting, coon dogs, coon-dog competition meets. I was curious because it had been such a big part of McElroy's life. The man had a stack of dog magazines on a table and gave me a couple to take, and he talked about the different breeds and how you trained them and hunted them. Kenny was one of the best, he said. He knew coon dogs. And he loved his dogs. But he would trade one or sell him for the right price.

We talked about dogs and Ken and Trena through the afternoon, and drank iced tea, until the light began to fade and I decided I needed to go while I could still find my way. I left with a stack of coon-dog magazines, a notebook full of notes—including a phone number—and an invitation to stop by again, any time.

I drove away as high as if I'd taken some exotic drug. I stopped in at a bar in the small nearby town for a beer to celebrate, and to imprint on my mind once again that you never ever knew about people. You knocked on every door; you dialed every phone number; you shook every hand. You assumed nothing. I jotted down notes.

My leg throbbed when I stood up to leave.

Jeffrey Dalsing, former Marshall David Dunbar and the author, in front the former post office, July 10, 2011.

CHAPTER 13

It was time to move the show out of Skidmore. I headed out of town east on Highway 113. Jeff and his friend followed close behind. I angled to the right on Highway V, and after a short distance turned right on Valley Road. Every time I had driven this road in the eighties I could imagine McElroy tearing down it in his pickup with a load of someone else's hogs or farm chemicals or on some errand of vengeance, clouds of dust trailing behind him. You went straight for a while and then came to a sharp curve and then passed the house where Tim still lived, just a hundred yards down the road from where McElroy's house once stood. I pointed out Tim's house to Jeff and slowed, to see if he wanted to stop in. I had suggested he might have better luck if he went one day without me. Over the years I had knocked on Tim's door several times, without response. Tim had a reputation of having been a terrific athlete in high school, and was thought to be embarrassed by his older brother's activities. I never heard a bad word about Tim.

We came to another slight bend in the road, and I pulled over. The empty space in front of us was where McElroy's house once stood. Several months after the killing, it was burned to the ground. No investigation was ever conducted. Through a grove of trees you could see a trailer. I had never determined who lived there, or who still owned the land, although I assumed it had been sold. I had walked the property more than once in my research. Looking for what, I was never sure—maybe a spent shell or two, a photograph, a pistol grip, some relic of what had gone on here. I had been looking, I suspect, for Ken McElroy himself.

Others asked me, and I asked myself, what caused him to be the way he was? Was he a sociopath? Crazy? I could never answer them in clinical terms, although he clearly had what you would now call an antisocial personality. But labels tell you nothing really. I could point to a range of facts: he was the thirteenth of fourteen kids, which meant he probably had to fight for his share of anything, including parental attention. His dad, Tony, was reputed to be loud and mean, a father who could be vicious in disciplining his kids. While the family had a decent piece of land, they existed on the poor end of the economic scale. Ken did badly in school, being held back grade after grade, which probably caused him to be picked on or ostracized by the other kids. He was filled with resentment at the way he thought people looked at him and his family. It ate at him; he couldn't let go of it. Once he placed you in the position of "the other," you were fair game: He could steal your pigs, your antiques, or farm chemicals; he could screw your wife, or rape your daughters; if it came to it he could shoot you in the stomach, or in the face.

The lawn in front of the trailer was nicely mowed. To the right grew lush rows of soybeans. The spot where the house had been had never fully grown in. It had been cleared of all signs of habitation. A telephone wire crossed the property. Beyond the site, the land was quite pretty, sloping off gently into planted farmland and deep timber. An old shed could be seen through a clump of trees. I never heard any names of those who burned down the house a couple of months after the killing. Some thought it had been done to rid the county of the ghost of Ken

McElroy; I wondered if it hadn't been done to stop the house from becoming some sort of shrine to the man. Perhaps a family member had done it.

I remembered coming out here one night long ago and lying down on the spot where the house had been, looking up in the face of a full moon in hopes that some understanding of McElroy might be divinely revealed to me. I wanted to feel him, through the soil on top of which he had lived. I drifted off, and awakened when a large cloud sailed in front of the moon and the night darkened.

The closest I came to an understanding of McElroy was a belief that he felt and saw slights everywhere, even as a little boy, and he could never let go of them—not one —so that they piled up and aggregated inside him as the fuel for a bottomless rage. And when Lois—a woman!— refused to sell him a pack of cigarettes it was every insult, every slight, real or imagined, he had suffered in his 47 years, and he was overwhelmed, taken over, consumed by a terrible rage that required vengeance or payback of a terrible sort. The harassing, the firing of a shotgun over Bo and Lois's house in the middle of the night, the following of her daughter in his truck, proved to be insufficient. Someone had to die, and they had to die at his hands. He drove around, and he waited, until one day he spotted Bo standing alone out on the loading dock, and it all came together. I saw him in some sort of crazed, almost transcendent state when he taunted the old man and finally reached in the window of his truck and lifted the shotgun from the rack.

Jeff stood on the spot where his father had lived. The trailer was barely visible through the trees behind him. His face was serious now, and I studied it for signs that he was feeling some connection with his blood father. I heard the dogs barking down the road at Tim's house, and I imagined the scene around this place, with the dogs and pickups and kids and women. We decided to move on.

Q Goslee never had a run-in with Ken McElroy, but he would have been the prototype of the farmer McElroy hated: fourth generation on the land, educated, successful, respected and admired in the community. Q and Margaret owned good land, and Q farmed it the way his father, grandfather and great-grandfather had. When Q said he thought it was time to put the seed in the ground, other farmers listened. When Q said he was thinking of spraying a new type of herbicide, others paid attention. Farmers studied the fields as they drove the countryside to see how others' crops were doing, if they were planted in a straight line, if the hills were yellow from lack of good topsoil. Q's fields were always among the best.

Q was the last one in the Goslee family to accept me. For months, he kept a wary eye as I came and went from his house and sat at his dinner table. He was pleasant and he joked, but he revealed little of what he knew or thought. Q got up every morning at 5:30, and headed into town for coffee at Mom's, along with many other farmers in the area—people he'd known all his life. One morning, after I'd been around for five or six months, I was awakened early by a knock on my bedroom door.

"Harry, you want to go into town for coffee?"

I was shocked. "Be right there," I said, jerking on my pants. I knew he wouldn't wait long for me. I hit the back door just as he was starting his pickup. He didn't say anything on the ride to town. As we got out of the truck and stepped up on the sidewalk, I couldn't help but remember the only other time I had come in here, over a year ago now, and what had happened then. I wondered what lay in store for me now. Q held the door for me, and I walked in.

The same thing happened. As eyes fell on me, the voices dropped. Then the faces turned to Q, right behind me, and I could sense the confusion. He walked over to the closest table, motioned me over, and said, matter-of-factly, something like, "You boys all know Harry don't you?" And that was all it took. Most mumbled "yes," or "yeah"; a few held out hands to be shaken. I took an empty seat across the table from Q. The conversation picked back up, and it was as if I'd been sitting there every morning for the past 20 years. From then on, I could walk in and sit at any table in the coffee shop.

From McElroy's house, Jeff and his friend and I proceeded in our cars down the old Valley Road until it swung back around and we passed Romaine Henry's farm. When I first visited Romaine, I figured I would run into a stonewall, but he had invited me in and we sat at the kitchen table and talked while his wife worked over the sink. At one point he pulled up his shirt to show me the scar from the blast of McElroy's shotgun. He wondered aloud how the jury could conclude that he didn't know who shot him. I asked Romaine why he thought McElroy shot him, and he shook his head and said he had no idea. I had heard rumors that he and McElroy were sleeping with the same woman, the wife of Henry's hired hand, but I had never been able to substantiate them.

We got back on Highway V and headed back into Maryville, where we ate lunch at a Mexican restaurant. There hadn't been any Mexican or Italian restaurants in Maryville when I hung around in the eighties. There were bars, a few local restaurants, and fast-food joints. Sometimes, after I had been running the back roads of northwest Missouri too long, staying in local motels of small towns 30 or 40 miles away—McElroy cut a wide swath—I would begin to feel cut off from civilization. There was a lack of newness, or stimulation, in the small towns that would get to me. Everyone seemed to be saying the same things; it was all about the weather and crop prices and the Kansas City Royals. The young and ambitious seemed to have all moved out and moved on. There were no movie theaters or playhouses. Even in Maryville, the culture was based on farming and all that went with it.

I would sometimes drive to St. Joe just to see a movie, or eat in a real restaurant. Once I checked into a motel and watched television all day just to distract myself from the place, from the seeming endlessness of the task.

One night, driving home after an interview with Trena's best friend in school, I realized I would not have a real story unless I talked to Trena. No one in Nodaway County knew where she was, and they didn't want to know. She had sued the town, alleging her husband's killing amounted to a violation of his civil rights, and eventually settled for $17,500. (Nodaway County paid $12,000; Del Clement paid $3,000; and Skidmore paid $2,000.) Richard McFadin, McElroy's lawyer, handled the case. He was my best shot.

When I first called McFadin for an interview, he insisted that there must be something in it for him. He was tired of giving interviews for nothing. I talked about journalistic integrity, and said I would write the book with or without him, and he was such a key part of the story that I really wanted to get his role right. I had counted on the fact that trial attorneys run on massive egos, and that the idea of his role being understated or misrepresented in the book would be intolerable. I was right, but I had no idea how right.

I drove to his office in Kansas City. We talked in his office for a while, and went to lunch. I could feel him sizing me up. I scribbled notes furiously when he said something witty or insightful. Back at his office, he looked at me for a moment, flipped through a book, and dialed a number.

"Trena," he said after a few seconds. "Gene McFadin.

Listen, I got a guy sitting across the desk from me that I think you should talk to. He'll make it worth your while." A week later I met her and her new husband at a small town in the Ozarks and interviewed her for longer than three hours. Journalistic integrity aside, I recall paying her four or five hundred bucks.

The other thing was the files. McElroy had been charged with crimes in counties all over northwest Missouri, including 12 charges of raping Trena when she was 12 and 13. Some of the court records were missing and some were sealed. There were also cases I had heard about but couldn't track down. There were all sorts of rumors about McElroy's contacts with the law, but few facts. I needed specifics to make the book hang together. After McFadin hung up with Trena, he called his secretary into the office and told her to set me up in the empty conference room with all of McElroy's files and a copy machine and give me anything else I needed. I was near speechless. This was stuff no one else had, or would ever get. It was in fact a richer trove than I had even imagined. I spent the next three days reading and copying files, making new lists of people to talk to, jotting down phone numbers and addresses next to their names. Every couple hours, scared that the rules would change, I would take the new material out to the car, put it in the trunk and lock it. I had enough new work for a year.

After lunch at the Mexican restaurant, we headed south to St. Joe to visit McElroy's grave. Jeffrey had visited the grave this morning on the way up to Skidmore, so I followed him through the gates of the cemetery, which were only a few blocks off the highway. It was past midday by the time we pulled to stop at the curb and stepped from the air-conditioned vehicles. The air was humid, and the sun was beating down hard. We parked, and walked a few feet to the brass plaque. In the upper corners were images of an open Bible. Beneath what looked like a flower holder were the raised, tarnished words: Beloved Ken. Beneath that was his full name:

Ken Rex McElroy Brave, Fearless and Compassionate "Beloved Ken." I remembered again what Trena had said when she faced the press a few days after the killing: "He never knelt down to nobody."

When I interviewed her in 1983, there was no trace of the angry, defiant Trena. She spoke in a soft voice, like the 12- or 13-year-old girl she had been when Ken captured her. She defended him but with little heart. The feeling I had was that it was for the benefit of his kids; for their sake she couldn't be heard saying their father was a monster. Her new husband stood close by and listened, but did not interfere or comment.

By all accounts Trena had been a shy, sweet girl before Ken got a hold of her. It felt like something of that person was emerging from the long nightmare of her adolescence. I remembered, at the interview, shaking her hand, looking her in the eyes for a moment, and realizing that I had no idea of what she had really been through. No one but she ever would. I felt a sense of gratitude that she was getting a second chance at life, and that this man—the seeming antithesis of Ken—was now at her side.

I doubted that she had designed this plaque in 1981. Maybe back then she came up with "brave" and "fearless," but not "compassionate." Was Ken McElroy brave? He had the town, the county—including the law—scared to death of him, but I wasn't sure that made him "brave." He never fought a man with his fists, as far as I knew. He relied on guns and threats. He was a master of intimidation, of instilling fear in others. But how brave is it to shoot an elderly man in the face with a shotgun? I sometimes wondered if there was in fact a balanced mind behind the mask, if he calculated that, by acting dangerous and unpredictable, he could master the town with fear.

Del Clement as a senior at Nodaway Holt high school in 1972. *Trena McCloud as a freshman in Nodaway Holt, the same year Del Clement was a senior. She knew who he was.*

"Fearless?" Perhaps. The one man he worried about was State Patrolman Richard Stratton, the only law officer willing to stand up to him at night on the back roads, but I'm not sure he feared him. It was more like he knew he had met his match. The lack of fear could be simply wound up in the paranoia and consuming rage.

"Compassionate"— that was a joke. Perhaps McElroy convinced Trena that he loved her in his own way, but no rational human being could believe that what he had done to her involved any sort of genuine caring. My guess was that he turned her head to see the world through his paranoid eyes, and when the effect of him finally wore off, and she saw the world through her own eyes, the past receded into darkness—a place where she no longer went.

I stood for a moment suddenly stunned by the scene at the grave. Thirty years to the day after Ken Rex McElroy was shot to death I was standing over his remains with one

74

of his children. It seemed like I had entered into some sort of myth. (This was, after all Jesse James country.) All civilizations have their myths, of gods and demons, of transgression and redemption, of good and evil, of great tragedy. It was truly a tragedy: A man without conscience terrorizing a small town into committing murder; Skidmore forever known as the vigilante town that took the law into its own hands when the law failed; good overcoming evil, but leaving great destruction in its wake. A myth showing us that civilization is mainly a matter of the consensus of the citizens, that once they no longer believe in the rule of law, it no longer exists.

Jeffrey knelt down by the grave, and I snapped his picture: the son gazing at his father's grave. He glanced up at me, and I saw his eyes, the father's eyes, gazing at me. I snapped another picture.

Our visit was over. We said our good-byes, got in our separate cars, and drove from the cemetery. Jeffrey and his friend headed south to Kansas City, and I swung north, back up to Skidmore, the scene of the crime.

CHAPTER 14

I couldn't say for sure how much time I spent in Skidmore. I usually drove out from Denver for a month or two at a time. Sometimes I flew into Kansas City, rented a car, and drove north, staying for a couple of weeks. But it was probably close to three years by the end. In some ways, the town began to feel more like home than home. I could drive the back roads without thinking. I went to community events as if I belonged. I rode combines with Kirby Goslee and drove grain trucks from the farm to the elevator. I went to the bars and dances with the locals. I mowed the grass at the Goslee farmhouse.

Even so, I never felt that I had moved from the outside to the inside. I never expected to. But I remember driving home one night from Maryville over the rolling hills and twisting roads and suddenly realizing that I would in fact get the story. It was as if I had crested a hill and could see down across the plains. For a glorious moment in time, I wasn't worried about how I would write the book or get it published. Whatever else happened, I would not head back over the plains to Denver without the story.

Cheryl Brown continued to be a valuable ally. She asked me if I would come to the Methodist church one Sunday morning and sell tickets to the Mother's Day Bazaar. I accepted of course, and the next Sunday I sat at a table outside the sanctuary in front of a change box and a pile of pink tickets. Most people, even those I knew, were a little surprised to see me there. But it wasn't until a couple stopped in front of me, curious looks on their faces, and asked who I was that I realized how bizarre the scene truly was. I shook their hands, and asked if I could stop by for a visit sometime the next week. What could they say? I was there Monday afternoon.

A new difficulty gradually arose. I didn't know when to stop the research. With every interview I learned something new; even someone who wasn't a player in the drama would give me something: the name of one of McElroy's early girlfriends, the name of the man who sold him the Silverado in Mound City, the name of the social workers who tried to help Trena escape. I was afraid that if I stopped following absolutely every lead, calling every number, stopping by every farm, I would miss a key fact that could weave a new thread, however slender, into the story.

So I sat down every morning at the breakfast table in the Goslee farmhouse with my notepad, and Kriss and I went over the list, adding new names, scratching off old ones, and then I would set out for St. Joe, or Ravenwood, or even Kansas City, in search of another person or piece of paper to help me unravel the many mysteries of the story. I also went back a second time, sometimes a third or fourth time, to talk to some people I felt had more to say.

I drove the countryside and talked into my tape recorder about what I was seeing: the monster combines, the farmhouses on hilltops, red-tailed hawks flying over the timber, the changing colors of the crops in the fields. I knew one day I would have to paint the scene, but I also found myself captivated by what I came to see as the transformation of the land through the seasons of planting, growing, and harvesting. Kirby Goslee, the farming son of the family, explained the technical aspects of farming to me and the complexity of the decisions that had to be made: when to plant, what sort of herbicide to use, when to go into the fields to get the crop out. In many ways, it came to seem as much an art as a science. In the end, a farmer might stick his finger in the earth to see if the ground was ready to plant. The changing hues of the land through the seasons came to seem like an evolving impressionistic painting.

I continued to dig around in the underworld. Since coon hunting had been such a big part of McElroy's life, I decided I needed to go on a hunt, preferably with some of his buddies. Kriss set it up. One spring night, out of season, we drove to an isolated farmhouse west of Skidmore, where two or three men awaited us in the yard. Most wore heavy beards and hats pulled down so you could barely see their eyes. In the back of the pickup was a case of beer, a jug of whiskey, and three shotguns. The men eyed me with suspicion, and when, to my consternation, Kriss explained that I was there to do some research for a book on Ken McElroy, I thought things were going to go bad quickly; one of the men jerked back as if slapped, another seemed to twitch toward one of the shotguns lying in the bed of the pickup.

"I need a drink," I said, and grabbing the jug I took a swill of stuff so cheap it burned my throat like lime. I clunked the bottle down, grabbed a beer, and swilled that in two long pulls. Eyes watering, on the verge of vomiting, I eyed each of the men in turn.

"Let's get us some fuckin' coon," one of them finally said, and we piled into two pickups. The second carried four dogs in cages. We drove into the night on back roads until I was totally confused as to where we were. The trucks finally pulled over alongside a fence; one of the men dropped the tailgate on the second truck and opened the cages. The dogs were wild. The men spoke to them, then turned them loose into the timber. We sat there and listened. The dogs howled and barked and yelped. We inched forward along the fence line. The men interpreted the language of the dogs, as if they were reading a book. "That's Blue, on the trail," or "Jed is taking off to the south," or, in response to a long howl, "That's Betsy, got one up a tree." The truck stopped, two men got out, and with shotguns in hand jumped over the fence and took off into the woods. I listened as the howling grew more frantic. Our guide drove for a mile or two, made a right turn and then a left, and stopped. In a few minutes, the men and the dogs emerged. The dogs were still wild, but there was no coon. The men gave no excuse, drank from the bottles in the back of the truck, and off we went for another hunt.

I have to admit that, nervous about the guns and the whiskey and the semi-crazed look in one of the men's eyes (whom I knew had been a close buddy of McElroy), I did not follow the men into the woods that night. I worried that it would be too easy for one of them to "stumble" across a log and discharge a gun in my direction.

CHAPTER 15

I finally found an agent for the book. And the agent finally found a publisher, HarperCollins (Harper & Row at the time). I got a minimal advance, but it gave me substantial credibility with people I wanted to interview to be able to say that I had a contract for the publication of the book.

I still had to produce a manuscript, of course, and I had a deadline of one year. The time finally came for me to transition from a researcher to a writer. I reviewed my material and wrote pages about the killing scene, or the countryside, or Trena, and sent it off to the editor. He was horrified, and after listening to him, so was I. The stuff was terrible.

Well, the actual writing of the book is another story, but in short, one day, after several months of writing stuff and throwing it away, I packed up my boxes of materials and headed off to Hawaii, where I stayed for three months with friends who had a magnificent house overlooking Kealakekua Bay on the Big Island. I woke up the first morning to the crashing of the waves on the rocks below, and saw quite clearly that the way to begin the book was with the killing itself. I wrote of Cheryl Brown looking out the back window of the grocery store and watching the men stream down the street to confront McElroy for the first and final time. From there the order of things began to fall into place.

Over the next year and half, I swung back and forth between writing and researching. I would see what facts were missing from a scene, or I would get a new idea for a scene, or I would simply lose the feel of the place, and I would drive out again, and cruise the country roads again, and go out knocking on doors again. Gradually the form of the book grew more distinct and the gaps fewer and fewer.

There were occasional odd moments when the reality of where I was, what I was doing, and how far I had come, smacked me in the head. For example, the Punkin' Show always culminated in a big dance. In 1985, the dance was held in a large Quonset hut just off the main street where the town machinery was stored. It had a cement floor and a wide door, which was kept open for the dance. A stage for the band had been constructed along one wall. By 9 p.m. the hut was full and the crowd was dancing to the country and western band. I was drinking peach schnapps in the parking lot with the mayor and a few other locals—the normal practice before such gatherings—when Cheryl Brown found me and reminded me that I had agreed to judge the dance contest. I pulled myself together and followed her to the stage, where over the sound system she announced the rules of the contest and the names of the three judges—herself, me, and one other man whom I can't recall. No one, including myself seemed to think it the least bit strange that I was one of the three judges.

I took my job seriously, watching the dancers swing by in front of the stage one after another, and chatting with Cheryl about who was who, who looked good on the floor. Then a fellow in a white cowboy hat danced by. He was wearing pressed jeans, a western shirt, and cowboy boots, and he was holding a pretty brunette in his arms. It was Del Clement. The shooter. The killer. The scene seemed so bizarre that I almost said something. I glanced at Cheryl, the other judge, and at Del himself, to see if anyone else got it. It all seemed normal to everyone else. I kept my mouth shut. As the white hat danced on by I could only restrain a smile that it had all come to this: The author sitting in judgment on the dancing abilities of the killer and his wife. Then his brother, Greg, and his wife danced by. Del made the cut down to the final three, but didn't win in the end. The last song was a two-step, and as I recall he and his wife danced well, but the other couple seemed more lively.

I returned to Skidmore from my visit to the cemetery in mid-afternoon. I stopped in front of the café and parked. The streets were empty as they would have been on July 10, 1981. Thirty years ago to this day, Ken Rex McElroy's reign of terror had been brought to a violent, bloody end. The men were back at their farms, McElroy's body was being prepared for an autopsy, and the law was organizing to go out and track down the killers. Alice and Trena and their many children were piling their belongings into pickups and preparing to leave, never to return.

After Ken McElroy's death, Trena moved to the Ozarks and remarried. She had five children by her new husband and by all account lived a happy, fulfilling life. She died of cancer Jan. 24, 2012.

National reporters who were in Kansas City for the collapse of the Hyatt Hotel bridge would soon receive word of the killing and would swarm up to Skidmore, only to be met by a wall of silence. They would already be shaping their stories about the "vigilante killing of the town bully." The town had no idea what lay ahead of it. One storm had passed, another was about to break.

The wind dropped. The place seemed deathly still, the way it must have seemed then. There was no town marshal in Skidmore now. Hadn't been one since the killing. No need, really. I thought back to what one of the lawmen had told me about the state of affairs in northwest Missouri the year before McElroy was shot. The word was out among law officers at all levels that if you found McElroy out alone on the roads at night, and if he had a gun with him—which was most nights—shoot him. Take him out. The law itself had turned lawless in the end.

AFTERWORD

HarperCollins published "In Broad Daylight" in 1989. The book won an Edgar Award for best True Crime and was a New York Times bestseller for 12 weeks. It sold more than one million copies in paperback.

The book was also made into an NBC Movie of the Week by the same name in 1994. It starred Brian Denehey as Ken McElroy, Marcia Gay Harden as Trena, Chris Cooper as Trooper Richard Stratton, and Cloris Leachman as Lois Bowenkamp. It was filmed in a small town outside of Austin, Texas, which bore little resemblance to Skidmore. I visited the set during the filming. Denehey played the death scene in the truck so subtly that it had me wondering again if McElroy had been asking for it. The movie still plays on cable channels.

In commemoration of the 25th anniversary of the shooting, St. Martin's Press reissued the book in paperback in 2006 with a new epilogue that brought the story up to date. I had gained access to many investigative documents that provided a great deal of new information about the identity of the killers, the killing itself, and the aftermath, which was included in the epilogue.

Trena died of cancer Jan. 24, 2012, while I was in the preparation of this manuscript. She lived with her husband, Howard, in a small town in southwestern Missouri, not far from her parents, Treva and Trena. She had five children by Howard and was a great-grandmother by age 54. By all accounts she led a happy life.

Others in the story have died as well: Bo and Lois Bowenkamp, Alice Wood, Pete Ward, Frankie Aldredge, Romaine Henry, Del Clement, and Richard McFadin, to name a few. Q Goslee died in 2009. I returned to Skidmore for his funeral. His wife, Margaret, is now 93.

David Baird, the country prosecutor who convicted McElroy in the Bowenkamp shooting in 1980, and who declined to prosecute Del Clement for McElroy's shooting, was re-elected to the position every four years until 2011, when he was defeated. He is now the prosecutor in an adjoining county.

The townspeople did not like the movie In Broad Daylight. They felt it did not truly portray what it was like living under the reign of terror visited upon their town by Ken Rex McElroy. Most of the residents like the book, though. To this day, strangers continue to drive through town, looking for the markers of the crime story. When locals are approached, some will say the story has been told in the book "In Broad Daylight," and they don't know anything more than what's in there.

I doubt the killers of Ken McElroy will ever be brought to justice. For one thing, Del Clement, the primary shooter, died of liver disease in 2009. To prosecute the men on the .22 and the shotgun would require consistent, corroborated testimony by at least two witnesses. The new prosecutor has even less reason than his predecessor did to reopen an investigation into the killing. The case, although officially open, is in fact closed.

Over the years I have debated the morality of the killing in many forums. I appeared, among many other venues, on "Oprah" and "Larry King Live." During the latter, Larry King pressed me on whether I thought the killing was justified. I responded the way I usually responded to that question: I believed that from the town's point of view there really was no other choice. The law had failed to protect the people; they were entitled to protect themselves. King pressed me on my personal belief, and I could only say that in those circumstances I understood why killing McElroy seemed the only rational course. After the show was over, he turned to me and said that in his mind it was never right to take a life outside of the law. Never. Maybe you would feel different, I said, if it was your daughter who was being raped or your parents who were being shot.

The rightness or wrongness of what happened on the morning of July 10, 1981, is a question that people will have to ponder and decide for themselves. What is clear is that the criminal justice system had broken down. The town was justified in its belief that the law could not, or would not, protect it from McElroy and that McElroy was bent on further mayhem. What is not so clear, however, is that the killing was something akin to a collective act of self-defense.

I believe that the decision to shoot Ken McElroy was not a rational act. Neither was it a group decision. It was a snap decision by two or three men who had been drinking that morning and decided they had finally had enough of Ken Rex McElroy. McElroy has simply pushed them one step too far. The men reacted by reaching for their guns. It was an impulse, not a decision. If they had thought about it, the killers wouldn't have shot McElroy in broad daylight, on the main street of town, in front of 45 witnesses, making each and every one of them, by their ensuing silence, accessories after the fact to murder.

Richard Stratton, the state patrolman who hunted McElroy down after the Bo Bowenkamp shooting, did not participate in the investigation. After Stratton arrested him, McElroy threatened him and his wife, in person, and it was felt that Stratton couldn't be objective in the pursuit of his killer(s). But he knew all of the investigators, and he had his belief about who was involved in the killing and how it went down.

When I knocked on the door of Stratton's house the first time, I assumed he, like many of the law officers in the story, would be reluctant to talk. To the contrary, he invited me in and we sat down and talked for longer than three hours. I came back several more times to confirm details, dig a little deeper into his recollections and perceptions, and talk to his wife, who had had her own encounters with Ken McElroy. When I had a draft of the manuscript ready, I asked him to read it, which he agreed to do. I wanted to know if the way I told the story was the way it was; if there was any credible theory out there that the primary shooter was someone other than Del Clement.

He called me after he read the draft. In that friendly but reserved way of his, he said, "You got it right, Harry. That's the way it happened."

The only person who was ever seriously put forward as the primary shooter of Ken McElroy was, in fact, Del Clement. Although I did not name him as the killer in "In Broad Daylight," I subsequently obtained additional convincing additional evidence against him from the police files, which is set forth to the epilogue to the 2007 paperback rerelease and e-book version of the book. For "The Story Behind 'In Broad Daylight'" I wanted a photo of Del. I had one of him in his white cowboy hat in a newsletter, but it was a little grainy. I wanted one of him as a young man.

On my last day in town on a visit in the fall of 2012, a classmate of Del's brought a copy of the 1972 Nodaway Holt yearbook to the Goslee farm. Del was a senior that year, and sure enough there was a head-and-shoulders photo of him as a fresh-faced lad, and another one of him as an actor in a play in makeup and dressed in full cowboy regalia, and a third as a member of the basketball team.

The fellow who brought the yearbook flipped a few pages and pointed to a smaller photo of a familiar face: Trena McCloud, as a freshman: pretty, open, innocent. I felt a shock of intense rage at Ken McElroy for what he was about to do to her, for the ruin he was about to visit upon this young girl, and for those who over the years who had told me what a good guy he really was.

Something else hit me: Trena was in high school at the same time as Del. She had to know who he was. There were only 120 kids in the school. People used to discount Trena's unwavering identification of Del as the shooter by saying she was just a kid and probably confused Del with someone else, maybe one of his four brothers. But the yearbook also showed that one of the brothers was in her class, and another was in the class behind her. She had been going to school with the Clement brothers for years. She knew who Del was. In those small towns, everybody knew everybody, and you sure would know the other kids in school.

Whatever doubt lingered in my mind as to who shot Ken McElroy was now erased. The photos of Del Clement, Ken McElroy's alleged killer, and Trena McCloud, McElroy's wife, only a few pages apart in the same yearbook, had finally convinced me. The man Trena saw raising the rifle to his shoulder and taking aim at her husband the moment before his head exploded was in fact Del Clement.

ABOUT THE AUTHOR

 Harry MacLean is a New York Times bestselling author and lawyer living in Denver, Colorado. He has written four books. He writes, arbitrates labor disputes and dreams of living by the ocean. MacLean graduated from the University of Denver College of Law, magna cum laude, and also received a master's degree in Law and Sociology from DU. He worked as a trial lawyer for the Securities and Exchange Commission and as a magistrate in Denver Juvenile Court. He taught as an Adjunct Professor at DU Law. He served as First Assistant Attorney General for the state of Colorado, and as General Counsel of the Peace Corp during the Carter Administration. For the past twenty years he has worked as a labor arbitrator and book author.

Connect with him at facebook.com/HarryNMacLean, twitter.com/HarryNMacLean, and www.HarryMacLean.com.

Other books by Harry MacLean

In Broad Daylight
A Murder in Skidmore, Missouri

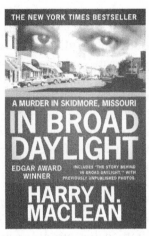

Harry MacLean's first book tells the story of the killing of a bully in a small town in northwest Missouri in 1981, in front of 45 witnesses. Explores Ken McElroy's reign of terror, his killing, and the cover-up which has protected the killer ever since. In Broad Daylight won an Edgar Award for Best True Crime, was a New York Times Bestseller for 12 weeks, and became a movie starring Brian Denehey in 1990.

The latest edition contains new facts on the killing and the identity of the killer.

Available in hardcopy, paperback, ebook, and audio.

www.harrymaclean.com/in-broad-daylight

The Joy of Killing
A Novel

In his classic works of true crime, Harry N. MacLean examined the dark side of America and its fascination with violence. In The Joy of Killing he builds upon this expert knowledge to create a page-turning literary thriller about the origins of violence.

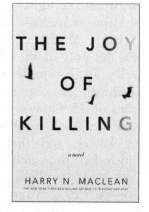

This fever dream begins on a stormy fall night in the north woods of Minnesota, where we meet a college professor who once authored a novel in which he justified a gruesome murder under the theory that there is no moral center to man's activity. Playing on a continuous loop in his mind are key moments in his past, centered around his fixation on an erotic meeting with a girl on a train bound for Chicago when he was just fifteen. All of these threads weave together as the writer tries to piece together the multitude of secrets that make up one human life.

Reminiscent of the work of noir master Derek Raymond and John Banville's The Sea with a touch of David Lynch, The Joy of Killing offers a searing, philosophical look at violence and its impact on our human condition.

Available in hardcopy, paperback, ebook, and audio.
www.harrymaclean.com/joy-killing

Once Upon A Time
A True Story of Memory, Murder and the Law

In 1989, Eileen Franklin, a young California housewife, claimed to recover a repressed memory of her father killing her playmate 20 earlier. In a landmark trial, the father was charged and convicted of first-degree murder, based solely on his daughter's testimony. This book chronicles the trial, explores the remarkably dysfunctional Franklin family, and delves into the reliability of repressed memory as evidence in court.

Once Upon a Time was selected as a New York Times Notable Book of the Year. The New York Times called it a "deceptively important work. . . a many faceted and important study. MacLean gives an account of the trial which is comprehensive yet suspenseful, enriched by his insights into the tactics and emotions of the opposing lawyers."

Steve Martini, author of Compelling Evidence, wrote: "A tragic but gripping story, and expertly crafted. Mr. MacLean has a positive talent for detail, and an obvious knowledge of the law. I congratulate him on a masterfully told story."

"Once Upon a Time" is also available as an e-book.
www.harrymaclean.com/once-upon-a-time

The Past Is Never Dead

The Trial of James Ford Seale and Mississippi's Search for Redemption

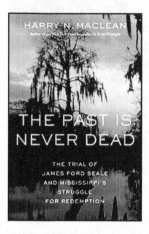

On May 2, 1964, Klansman James Ford Seale picked up two black hitchhikers and drowned both young men in the Mississippi River. Seale spent more than forty years a free man, before finally facing trial in 2007. There could have been two defendants in the resulting case: James Ford Seale for kidnapping and murder, and the State of Mississippi for complicity—knowingly aiding, abetting, and creating men like Seale. In The Past Is Never Dead, best-selling author Harry MacLean follows Seale's trial, the legal difficulties of prosecuting kidnapping and murder charges decades after the fact, and the strain on a state contending with a past that can't be forgiven. MacLean's narrative is at once the account of a gripping legal battle and an acute meditation on the possibility of redemption.

Published by Basic Books, "The Past Is Never Dead," was shortlisted for the William Saroyan Award, given by Stanford University.

www.harrymaclean.com/the-past-is-never-dead

Made in the USA
Monee, IL
27 August 2020

39479459R00059